I0821658

THE Pueblo Food Experience COOKBOOK

THE

The Pueblo Food Experience

COOKBOOK

Whole Food of Our Ancestors

EDITED BY

Roxanne Swentzell and Patricia M. Perea

Original drawings by Roxanne Swentzell

Flowering Tree Permaculture Institute

Museum of New Mexico Press
Santa Fe

We would like to dedicate this book to our Ancestors.
For without their hard work and amazing survival skills,
we would not be here today.
We thank them for their love, wisdom, and guidance.
Ku-da-wah-ha

CONTENTS

ACKNOWLEDGMENTS

I WOULD LIKE TO ACKNOWLEDGE the individuals who made the Pueblo Food Experience (PFE) project possible. It could not have happened without all those in the first diet group who so bravely agreed to go through the three-month trial period. Their perseverance and willingness to share their health conditions and blood tests with the world proved without a doubt that we were on the right track. First, I want to thank my son, Porter Swentzell, for testing the waters and doing much of the research to give us a starting point. Marian Naranjo for being such a spiritual force, keeping us on the right track of our journey. Chastity Sandoval for changing her eating so radically during those months that she inspired many after they heard her story. Jonathan Loretto for jumping on board and sticking to it, all the way from Cochiti Pueblo. Patricia Reifel, who made the change permanent. I could always count on her showing up to potlucks and gatherings. Nate Fuentas, who proved you could eat this way even when traveling the world. Louie Hena for holding the prayer in Tesuque Pueblo. For my grandchildren (Ailani, Eleseo, and Emiliano) who did without ice cream and cookies and instead learned how to make cactus juice and tortillas—Grandma thanks you. Annette Rodriquez for trying it and sharing her story. Raymond Naranjo for his amazing dishes. Nathana Bird, Beata Tsosie, Samuel Catanach, Roger Fragua, Rose Simpson, Dylan McLaughlin, Karl Duncan, Karen Cantor, Dr. Maria Gabrielle, and Susan Gazette for their support and interests.

I also want to thank Patricia Perea and Lisa Pacheco for working with me to produce this book so that others can learn what is possible. Funding for the Pueblo Food Experience came from the Chamiza Foundation, the Santa Fe Community Foundation, Silicon Valley Institute, and a donation from my mother, Rina Swentzell.

Roxanne in kitchen cleaning wild spinach, 2014 *(opposite)*

For those who have come to our talks or brought us squash, corn, beans, and meat, I thank you, for it most certainly takes a whole community to make us all healthier.

—Roxanne Swentzell

IT IS HARD TO BELIEVE that a little more than two years have passed since Roxanne and I sat down in her library and talked about what a Pueblo Food Experience cookbook might look like. I am so grateful that we have been able to see this project through to the end. I thank Roxanne for allowing me to work on this project with her. I would also like to thank Lisa Pacheco for her dedication to the project. Her work and energy have been priceless throughout this entire process. I am also grateful for Dr. Irene Vasquez, who gave me the opportunity to return to the University of New Mexico, where I was able to expand our cookbook's audience. I have been consistently welcomed and embraced by Roxanne and her family. Without Porter, Chastity, and Rose, my short stay in Chimayó would not have been as full and beautiful as it was. And although it has been many years since my grandparents Jacobo Velasquez Perea and Dominga Olguin Perea passed, the food the three of us shared often made its way into this cookbook. This is also true of my grandmother Viola Lomas and my grandfather Juan Alonzo, whose crockpot beans surpass anything else I have ever tasted.

As always, I am thankful for my dad, George Perea, and his ingenious way of making incredible food out of apparently random and incompatible ingredients. Dad also inspired many conversations about the preparation of buffalo during this project. As I was growing up, my mom, Norma Perea, never let an illness go by without putting corn tortillas in the frying pan and serving up my brother Adrian and I caldo with half cobs of corn floating in the broth. To this day, her *caldo* (soup) is the best I have tasted. And, of course, boundless thanks go to Annette Rodriguez, who came home excited by the Pueblo Food Experience and committed herself to the indigenous recipes and ingredients for every meal she made in our home. Her butternut squash soup is out of this world, and its taste reminds me why I have chosen to spend my life with her.

Finally, as this book project comes to a close, I reflect on one of the many conversations Roxanne and I had about these recipes. They really are simple—the food we all grew up with, the food that was the cheapest and most available. Our intention with this cookbook is to remind our communities that the food we have often taken for granted is the food that takes the best care of us.

—Patricia M. Perea

INTRODUCTION

Roxanne Swentzell

SOMETIMES, WHEN WE ARE limited by circumstances, our creative humanness rises to the occasion. This seems true with me. I was born into a time and place that held many conflicting forces, so it was easy to get swept away by the mainstream society and hard to figure out how to hold onto my unique identity and honor my existence.

As a Native American woman, born between worlds and in a time of great environmental changes, I found myself inspired to learn new old ways—ways of not only surviving but also creating a meaningful life. In the 1980s, I was privileged to be introduced to permaculture. I remember a conversation with Bill Mollison about how he came up with the name *permaculture*. He spoke about it being two words combined: *permanent* and *culture*—permaculture—the permanence of culture. I had no idea at the time that my journey into permaculture would lead me backward, or rather, deeper into what culture is.

Like most permaculturists, we were interested in creating a sustainable homestead based on the models of Nature. Joel Glanzburg, my husband at the time, and I cofounded Flowering Tree Permaculture Institute and spent the next ten years creating a homestead that could feed a family of four and an array of different farm animals. We grew a "food forest" on one-eighth of an acre of high desert in northern New Mexico. We taught classes on farming, animal husbandry, food storage, pottery, you name it—anything that had to do with hands-on survival skills. The more we learned, the more there was to learn. Just like our small yard: the more we added, the more complicated the system became, so what was once a very small piece of dry wasteland became whole ecosystems that multiplied with each new species of plant, animal, insect, bird, fish, worm, or fungus. That one-eighth of an acre became a deep, rich

Roxanne harvesting corn, 2014 *(opposite)*

Flowering Tree Seed Bank, Santa Clara Pueblo, 2015

forest of unbelievable diversity and life within its many layers. I feel overwhelmed and small within it.

Watching it evolve over thirty years, I've learned some things about "culture" that I apply directly to myself. Not everything prospered in the environment of the yard. The microclimates, species, and planned design methods were not always the answer to success. The situation was far more complicated than any plan our human brains could create. I didn't know at the time that I was watching a family evolve based on belonging to a place.

What did not "belong" died or struggled endlessly to remain. I watched this orchestra struggle from making just noise into playing something that sounded like music. I realized that Nature is doing this dance always. If you leave it alone long enough, it will balance into a most harmonious culture of life. People forget that they do the same. We think we can go anywhere and do anything our minds think up. We forget that we are part of the family of life on earth and that some places and conditions fit together better than others. I define *culture* as that which belongs to a place and a way of life because it has been formed by, and it has formed, what surrounds it over long periods of time. A culture takes time to form. Even cultures in a petri dish take time to grow.

Our seed bank was a constant reminder of where we were. Only certain plants—mostly our Pueblo crops—thrived in this high desert landscape. As a Native person myself, I was already interested in the preservation of Native crops and lifeways, but I hadn't put it all together quite yet. I was still in the mind-set of being a seed saver or a permaculturist or a farmer or a teacher. I wasn't seeing myself in the context of culture. Yes, I thought of myself as a Native person partaking in community activities once in a while, but I wasn't seeing how I was part of the ecosystem of a larger cultural belonging that involved my local surroundings and my DNA. We are a species that thrives or doesn't because of being in the right place or the wrong place.

I became obsessed with how it all fit together. I had been saving our traditional crops for years; I stored most of them away just to save the seeds from extinction. I bought organic products from natural food stores. I struggled with weight and health issues and never seemed to find real help—just excuses and more Band-Aid remedies. My son, Porter, is a historian, and we talk a lot about our common interests. One year he researched what exactly our ancestors ate before the introduction of European foods. He decided to eat that way for a few months to see if you could still do it in modern times. Yes, you can.

But something happened that we didn't expect. Putting the environment and us together created a profound thing. Some unexpected "fit" started a domino effect of health, not just in our physical bodies but also in our spiritual lives and lifestyle. I realized that we, the people of this landscape, needed to find our right place again in the system. I once read that it takes twenty generations in the same location for a species (humans included) to genetically adapt to that environment. The Pueblo Food Experience was the result of this experiment.

It is a project designed to help us remember where we fit in the permanence of culture. A group of Native people (whose ancestors have lived in northern New Mexico for more than twenty generations) agreed to eat only their original foods for three months. They took blood tests before and after the project. The results proved that we were doing the right thing. Everyone got healthier, and the diet

Emiliano holding cactus fruit, 2014

seemed to spur inspiration to change our lives for the better. The project was self-empowering. As a permaculturist, I love how this approach could save us in a time when we might have to find new ways to survive without our beloved grocery stores and fast food. We just might have to learn to feed ourselves again and to once again make things with our hands.

If our economy dried up tomorrow, if the stores closed, what could you make to eat with the resources you have now? This thought has always led me back to my ancestors, who were the true permaculturists of this arid Southwest. They figured out how to live sustainably in this environment for thousands of years. I look to them for answers. We got lazy and depressed and took all the easy handouts and forgot who we were and where we came from. There is a scary price for easy food—fast food is killing us, and I don't just mean McDonald's and Dairy Queen. I mean all the packaged foods in stores and all the unknown processed ingredients. There has been no cornmeal thrown for the lives taken. There have been no harvest dances for gratitude for the rain on our fields. There have been no prayers of thanks along the food's journey to our tables. Our connection to food is part of who we are as Native people, and when we disconnect from it, we are lost and easily tricked into buying whatever corporate greed dictates. The result is more than bad health; it is blindness and starvation of the soul.

The Pueblo Food Experience helped pave the path back to ourselves. It has been a long walk back to Mother Earth, but each piece of the puzzle we figure out is one more piece of ourselves that we have taken back from those who would wish us gone.

It is empowering to connect with any part of our surroundings. It is empowering to make something to eat from scratch from what is available in our environment. Growing food ourselves is also empowering. Walk instead of drive once in a while. Fix something yourself and see how it works or how you could make it better. We ourselves truly are the ones we have been waiting for! This book was one of the outcomes of our journey. We wish to share this journey with others who want to really know how we fit and dance within the mystery of life, time, and place—within "the story of us."

A HISTORY OF PUEBLO FOOD

Porter P. Swentzell

PUEBLO PEOPLES AND THEIR ANCESTORS have long called the North American Southwest their home. This region includes the southern tip of Nevada, most of Utah, the southwestern section of Colorado, all of Arizona, all but the eastern edge of New Mexico, and most of the Mexican states of Sinaloa, Sonora, and Chihuahua. Defining factors of the Southwest include its watersheds, elevation, climate, plants, and animals.

In many ways, the Southwest could be characterized as the place of two major watersheds, the Colorado and the Rio Grande. The Colorado River, with its major tributaries the Green, San Juan, Little Colorado, and Gila Rivers, served as the key watershed for most Ancestral Pueblo people before the 1300s and for modern Hopi and Zuni peoples. After the 1300s, the Rio Grande watershed, with its major tributaries the Chama, Rio Puerco, Rio Conchos, and Pecos, served as a lifeline for eastern Pueblo peoples. Both watersheds have supported people, plants, and animals for untold generations.

The Southwest is marked by dramatic changes in elevation, from a mere 100 feet above sea level in the western basins to nearly 14,000 feet at the tops of some southern Rocky Mountain peaks. Western and southern parts of the Southwest tend to be at lower elevations and are defined by basins and ranges, while the northern portion of the Southwest contains high plateaus and the jagged Rockies. The eastern edge of the Southwest slides into the Great Plains. To the south are the rugged occidental and oriental Sierra Madre ranges, dividing Mexico east and west. The dramatic changes in elevation led to the development of distinct kinds of plants and animals in the Southwest, thus altering subsistence patterns for humans. Elevation has also impacted climatic conditions in the Southwest.

Harvest, Santa Clara Pueblo, New Mexico, ca. 1900 (NMHM/DCA 004128) *(opposite)*

The climate of the Southwest has changed dramatically over the last thirty thousand years. However, almost all of the Southwest has been arid during the past five thousand years or so. This is the time that Pueblo peoples became ethnically distinct from other indigenous peoples in North America. Climate is closely related to elevation, higher areas having colder winters and receiving more moisture in the form of snow and lower elevations having relatively mild winters and receiving almost all precipitation as rain. In addition to watersheds, precipitation has been a key source of life in the Southwest. The northwestern portion of the Southwest receives most of its precipitation in two distinct periods: winter and summer. Most precipitation in the southeastern part of the Southwest comes during summer months.

Wild plants and animals found in the Southwest are divided by elevation and climate. In general, higher elevations feature increased diversity in trees and large mammals, while lower elevations contain greater diversity in grasses, shrubs, and small mammals. Plants that grow at lower elevations are different from those that grow at higher elevations, due to differences in the harshness of winters. Watersheds serve as a haven for many kinds of riparian plants and trees, along with different animals and waterfowl. Multiple species of migratory birds stop in the Southwest or use its areas as seasonal homes during their annual travels.

The Gatherers

Before 2100 BCE, all humans in the Southwest survived by gathering plants and animals. The hunter-gatherer way of life was not a random daily search for edible things, but an organized, deliberate, and well-thought-out subsistence pattern known as the seasonal round. Small groups of people migrated from place to place based on season and corresponding food availabilities. The diets of gatherers were diverse, as many kinds of foods were eaten in a given year, although certain foods could be relied on almost exclusively at certain times. The following hypothetical example of this lifestyle is useful for understanding the diet.

Mary E. Dissette, detail of *Boy holding bird, San Ildefonso Pueblo, New Mexico*, ca. 1900 (NMHM/DCA 003753) *(left)*

Ailani holding jar of piñons, 2015 *(right)*

A group of gatherers moves from their winter base camp in the foothills down to a perennial stream in the spring to conduct their annual fish drive, when hundreds of pounds of fish are caught and eaten. This diet is supplemented by late spring and early summer greens.

As the warmth of summer takes hold, grass seeds for roasting and eating are harvested from meadow areas surrounding the perennial stream. With the arrival of the monsoons, the group moves from the floodplains to upland areas to dig for roots and to conduct pronghorn antelope drives. This food lasts them into the fall months.

Well before the onset of winter, the people locate their winter camp in the foothills below the mountains. The location of this winter village will change from year to year based on the availability of piñon nuts in any particular area. The rich nutritional value of piñon nuts can be easily supplemented by nearby mule deer and mountain sheep. As can be seen, this diet relied on multiple food sources and strategies.

The Coming of Corn

The earliest evidence for corn in the Southwest was found near modern-day Zuni Pueblo and was dated to 2100 BCE (Cordell and McBrinn 2012). Corn, or maize, was domesticated in Mesoamerica (present-day southern Mexico and most of Central America) approximately ten thousand years ago (Gremillion and Piperno 2009; Piperno

Fields at Shumopovi Pueblo, Hopi, Arizona, 1923 (NMHM/DCA 066743)

and Pearsall 1998). It took nearly six millennia, through countless generations of adaptation, for corn to reach the Southwest. Strains that were able to survive with limited moisture and short growing seasons eventually made their way into Pueblo country.

Maize did not initially have a major impact on Ancestral Pueblo peoples, probably for a number of reasons. First, the maize that initially came to the Southwest had much smaller yields than later strains. So maize was only one minor food source among many that gatherers used. Second, early horticulturalists may have been hesitant to invest too much labor in a food source that could be risky due to unforeseen events and circumstances (such as crop failure and environmental disasters). Third, full digestion of the nutrition in maize is limited by its lack of the amino acid lysine. This means that maize must be paired with protein such as meat, legumes, nuts, or seeds to be fully nutritious. Finally, maize-growing knowledge might not have been available or sought out by all groups in the Southwest.

After maize, other important crops made their appearance in the Southwest. Squash and amaranth made their way into Pueblo country by around three thousand years ago, and common beans by

Williamson, *Jemez woman (Ma-na) washing wheat, Jemez Pueblo, New Mexico,* 1936 (NMHM/DCA 042075)

about twenty-five hundred years ago (Cordell and McBrinn 2012). The appearance of these crops probably had an important impact on the value of corn. All of them include lysine, thus making maize more nutritious if eaten in conjunction. It is not surprising that agriculture began to take on increasing importance in the Southwest with the arrival of these crops. With the increase of the importance of agriculture came increasing sedentism and more elaborate pithouse architecture.

The Planters

About fifteen hundred years ago, Pueblo people began to rely increasingly on agriculture for food. They spent more of their time living near their fields in permanent pithouses. Harvested maize, beans, and squash needed to be preserved and stored until the next crop could be harvested. This need led to the construction of granaries and storerooms. Aboveground storerooms and special grinding rooms began to appear in the northern parts of the Southwest. These small groups of rectangular rooms surrounding pithouses were the predecessors of the later Pueblo villages. In some areas, increasing reliance on agriculture led to the construction of irrigation systems. Some comprised small catchments for redirecting natural flows, while others, like Hohokam systems, consisted of complexes of large canals running for many miles. Agriculture did not change just the material culture of southwesterners. It also significantly impacted culture in general.

Many peoples of the Southwest, like other agriculturalists in the Americas, venerated the crops that became so important during this period. This is especially true of maize. All parts of the maize plant were used for important everyday and cultural purposes. These agricultural products were increasingly relied upon for life itself. As a result, people in the Southwest have often spoken of maize as an extremely important supernatural being or even as a creator. During this time, agriculture grew into the core of the becoming of Pueblo people.

The Traders

Networks of exchange between different human groups have existed in the Southwest since time immemorial. Corn, beans, squash, amaranth, cotton, gourds, and other crops may have made their way into the Southwest through means of exchange. About one thousand years ago, centers of exchange in northern Mexico, in the Gila and Salt River watersheds, and in the Chaco Canyon region flourished. Pueblo architecture transformed as pithouses became more specialized (becoming kivas) and daily life centered more on the aboveground buildings. Large community structures called great houses, where many people may have gathered, were built at Chaco Canyon. Centers like Chaco Canyon, Paquime, and Casa Grande may have served as important places for the exchange of shells, turquoise, and macaws. Agricultural abundance may have facilitated these exchanges.

Nonfarmers living on the Southwest borderlands may have been interested in exchanging food items, thus carrying on a tradition

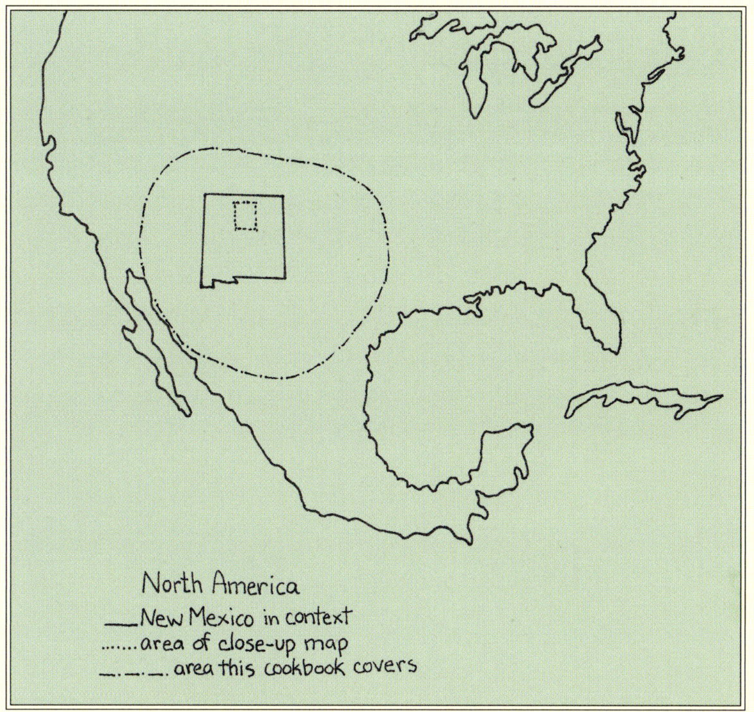

that had begun in the distant past. Gatherers from the Plains or the Great Basin exchanged food and other materials (especially those that were rare in the Southwest) for southwestern agricultural products. Plains peoples often brought bison meat, hides, and tools, along with nuts and grass seeds from farther east, to exchange for corn, pottery, and woven goods. This was true even after major migrations of people in the Southwest.

Between 1150 and 1450 CE, a series of events transformed the Southwest. Droughts and changes in weather patterns influenced the movement of people away from areas such as Chaco Canyon, Mesa Verde, and the Hohokam towns. By the 1300s, most Pueblo people were centered along the Rio Grande and its tributaries, while other populations lived in the Zuni area and on the Hopi mesas. This migration likely changed some of the networks of exchange, but many of the same food resources continued to move between the high and low deserts, the Great Basin, and the Plains. The biggest change in diet following the adoption of agriculture would come from an entirely new group of people.

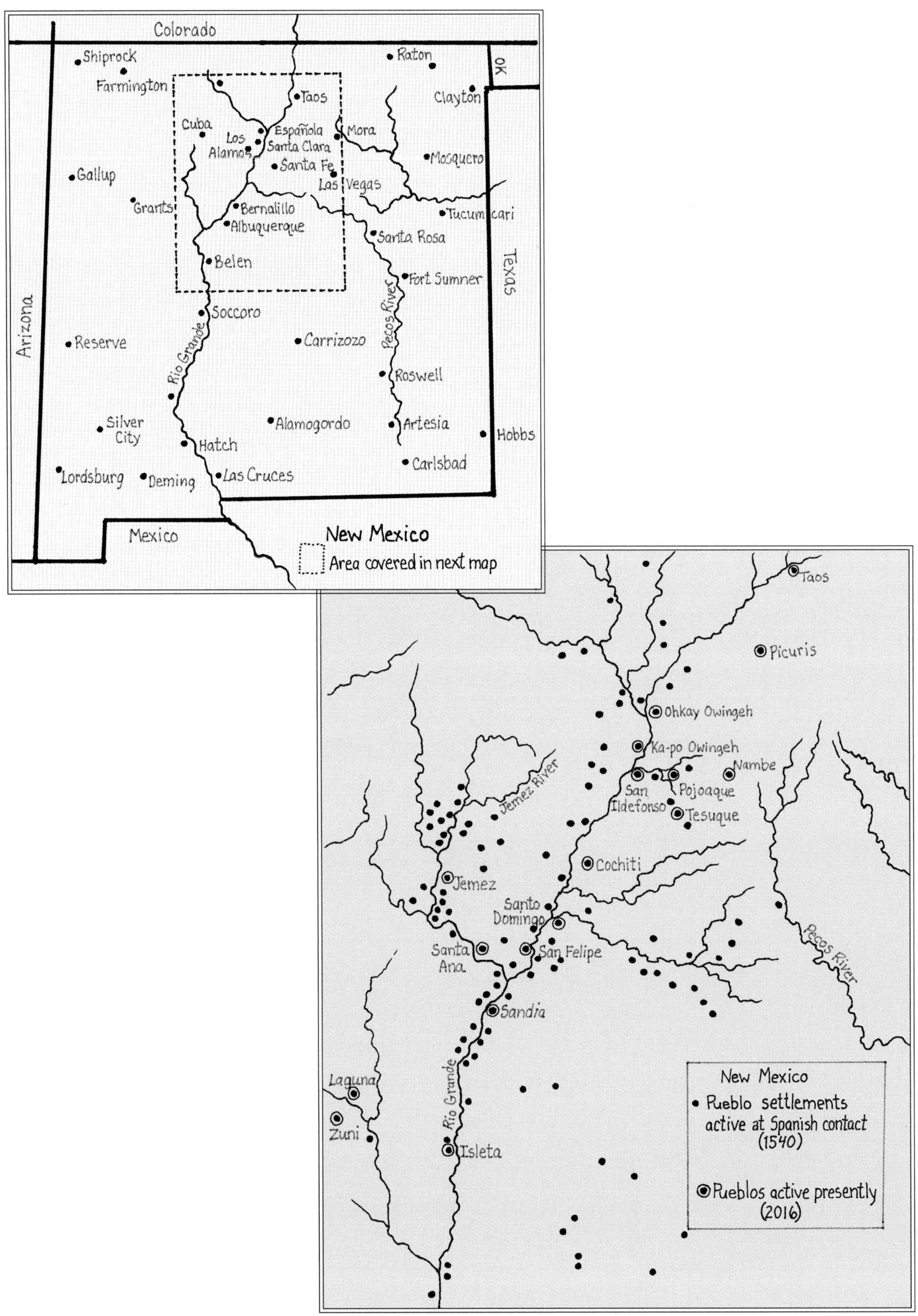
Colorado
Shiprock
Farmington
Raton
OK
Taos
Clayton
Cuba
Los Alamos
Española
Santa Clara
Mora
Santa Fe
Mosquero
Gallup
Las Vegas
Grants
Bernalillo
Albuquerque
Tucumcari
Santa Rosa
Belen
Fort Sumner
Texas
Arizona
Soccoro
Reserve
Carrizozo
Pecos River
Rio Grande
Roswell
Silver City
Alamogordo
Artesia
Hobbs
Hatch
Carlsbad
Lordsburg
Deming
Las Cruces
Mexico
New Mexico
Area covered in next map
Taos
Picuris
Ohkay Owingeh
Ka-po Owingeh
Nambe
San Ildefonso
Pojoaque
Tesuque
Jemez River
Cochiti
Jemez
Santo Domingo
Santa Ana
San Felipe
Pecos River
Sandia
Laguna
Zuni
Rio Grande
Isleta
New Mexico
Pueblo settlements active at Spanish contact (1540)
Pueblos active presently (2016)

The Coming of the Spanish

When Juan de Oñate and his motley group of colonists invaded the Southwest in 1598, they brought new items of exchange. Their invasion had been preceded by several groups of Spanish intruders, but this was the first group that stayed permanently in Pueblo country. As with the earlier expeditions, the Oñate group brought new animals: horses, donkeys, mules, oxen, sheep, goats, chickens, and pigs. They also brought new agricultural crops: wheat, barley, oats, melons, fruit trees, and many new vegetables. The Spanish came with auxiliaries, porters, and servants from multiple indigenous groups in Mexico, who also brought their local foods. Possibly one of the most important foods brought from Mexico was chile.

The establishment of the Spanish colony in New Mexico coincided with a period of unusual cold and short growing seasons. This led to massive food shortages and nearly caused abandonment of the colony. As Spanish farmers struggled to grow the crops they had brought with them, they relied on the Pueblos for food and animal feed. It became clear that the Spanish would have to primarily use local crops that had been acclimated to local conditions, supplemented by the food crops they had brought with them. Many of the new crops would eventually adapt to the Southwest and be grown by both Spanish and Pueblo peoples.

Pueblo people were introduced to the new crops primarily through the mission program. Franciscan missionaries built nearly sixty missions in the first thirty years of the colony. Each mission was tasked not only with the conversion of Pueblo people but also with being a self-sufficient base of Spanish culture. The missions relied on Pueblo labor for construction, maintenance, farming, and herding. This work became the initial process by which Pueblo people learned about tending orchards, growing melons, beekeeping, and animal husbandry. Some missions became specialists at producing certain kinds of food. For example, wine was very important for Catholic ritual, and some pueblos became well-known for their vineyards. However, Pueblo forced labor for these projects was a key factor leading to the Pueblo Revolt of 1680.

Led by Po'pey and others, nearly all pueblos rose up in rebellion against the Spanish in 1680. It was clear that the missions were key targets of the revolution; almost every mission was destroyed and many Franciscans were killed. Po'pey advocated that Pueblo people should eliminate all things Spanish, including food, from their lives. While some Pueblo people followed this instruction, many had become accustomed to the new foods, animals, and tools and did not want to get rid of them. It was clear that the new foods were here to stay.

During the two and a half centuries of Spanish rule in the Southwest, there wasn't much outside influence. The viceroyalty of New Spain restricted trade with other groups of Europeans, and the northern provinces were far from major trade centers. Many systems of exchange that had existed prior to the arrival of the Spanish continued with the new crops, although this trade was often interrupted by violence and captive taking. Piñon nuts and dried fruit were highly desired trade items. Mexican independence from Spain opened up the borders of the Southwest to Anglo-American traders and a new set of trade goods.

The Coming of the Anglo Americans

Anglo Americans took over most of the Southwest as a result of the Mexican-American War in 1848. Many Anglo traders had already made inroads into Pueblo country before the war, but now the Santa Fe Trail was fully opened to an influx of goods. The most impactful new items were building materials and tools such as metal grinders and, later, threshing machines. These machines and technologies made growing and harvesting wheat much easier, although the items did not reach Pueblo people very extensively or quickly (Vlasich 2005). As Anglo influences took hold, the predominant grain for many Puebloans shifted from corn to wheat. Wheat, combined with affordable mass-produced lard, led to "Pueblo bread" baked in *hornos*, considered part of the "traditional" diet in many pueblos today.

Anglo Americans also brought new canned foods. Over time, these would have an ever greater impact on the Pueblo diet as they became part of food supplies given to Native Americans by the US government. Also, many Pueblo people were introduced to Anglo

Ferenz Fedor, *Husking corn, Jemez Pueblo, New Mexico, ca.* 1940–1950 (NMHM/DCA 100295) *(opposite top)*

Santa Clara women harvesting corn, 2014 *(opposite bottom)*

foods at Indian boarding schools starting in the late 1800s. Pueblo children were often served coffee, toast, and wheat gruel at meals and were taught how to prepare Anglo-style recipes as part of their vocational training. Despite these introductions, many Pueblo people went back to their traditional crops and food sources after returning home.

The Modern Diet

World War II was a watershed event in Pueblo history and diet. Large numbers of Pueblo people served in the war effort: in the armed forces, in industry and at ports, and in Victory Gardens. Many learned new skills during the war, and afterward through the GI Bill and, later, relocation programs. World War II saw a rapid decline in sustenance agriculture in many pueblos as people turned to wage labor to survive (Vlasich 2005). Others looked to ranching for a livelihood, and fields that once grew food for people were turned to growing animal feed.

The change to wage labor meant that greater and greater proportions of food came from government commodities or from grocery stores. This trend continued through the twentieth century and reached its maximum extent in the twenty-first century, when each pueblo grew only a small proportion of its food. The radical change in diet has had a tremendous negative impact on health. Pueblo people have extremely high levels of diabetes, heart disease, and stroke compared with the wider US population. Health was identified as one of the critical concerns during the 2012 Pueblo Convocation, which gathered Pueblo people from all the different communities.

REFERENCES

Cordell, L. S., and M. E. McBrinn. *Archaeology of the Southwest.* 3rd ed. Walnut Creek, CA: Left Coast Press, 2012.

Gremillion, K. J., and D. R. Piperno. "Human Behavioral Ecology, Phenotypic (Developmental) Plasticity, and Agricultural Origins: Insights from the Emerging Evolutionary Synthesis." *Current Anthropology* 50, no. 5 (2009): 615–620.

Piperno, D., and D. M. Pearsall. *The Origin of Agriculture in the Lowland Neotropics.* San Diego: Emerald Group Publishing, 1998.

Vlasich, J. A. *Pueblo Indian Agriculture.* Albuquerque: University of New Mexico Press, 2005.

A SALT TRIP

Patricia M. Perea

AS WE DRIVE SOUTHEAST off the mesa, Porter tells us to turn around. We do. Black volcanic rock underlines the shadows of the Sandias as they lean into the sunrise. "Those rocks," Porter says, "are full of writing." On those rocks are warnings the Pueblos of the Rio Grande posted to the Comanche: *Stay to the east. We are here. This part of the world belongs to us.*

We pause. The sun has only just risen, yet it is already hot. It is the middle of July, and where we are going will only be hotter and drier. We continue to drive. Soon we are in Moriarty; the vast llano stretches out in front of us.

"The salt lakes are about two hours away," Roxanne tells us as she passes out ziplock bags full of homemade trail mix. We laugh as she holds up a freezer bag full of boiled turkey eggs. These are the things mothers do.

Moving south away from I-40, toward the vast stretches of the Chihuahua desert, the landscape completely changes. There are no mountains, no natural rivers or cultivated acequias. It's flat, endless, and beautiful. Thirty minutes into the desert and the sky is no longer deep turquoise. It is a color between blue and white, bleached and sometimes blinding. The plant life that surrounds us is short, thick, and unfriendly—cacti and creosote twist themselves into shapes of solid beings.

I lean into the window of the van. To so many, this land is desolate and ugly. It does not have the romance of northern New Mexico. There are no ancient cottonwoods or small, quaint mountain villages. But this is my home. I grew up in the vast expanse of these plains. Here, there are things we do not know how to see. Underneath this deceptively dry earth, water lies quiet and powerful. It seeps up into plants and makes the tastiest dirt I've ever known. Yes, tasty. Wet earth here tastes clean, like fresh clay.

Underneath us is the Estancia Basin. East of us is the little that is left of the once great Ogallala Aquifer, the source of water for our indigenous ancestors from the Dakotas to the eastern New Mexico plains. I've tasted that water too.

Today our mission is to gather what the ancient water left behind—salt. We are following the paths of those who came before to gather life-giving salt. We are in search of the mineral that keeps our cells alive.

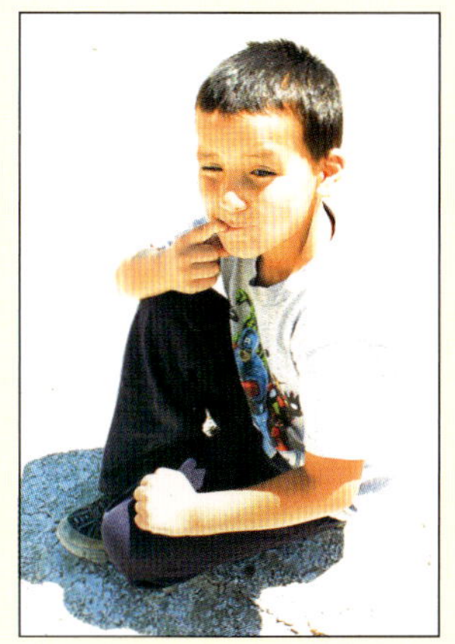

Emiliano tasting dirt, looking for salt, 2013

The salt lakes of New Mexico's Estancia Basin are not well-known to many, but for the indigenous people of New Mexico, they are a critical part of our historic migrations. And that is what we are doing on this punishingly hot and bright July day—we're migrating south like so many of those who came before us. We're moving now. We have always been moving. Life is not still.

Just to the west of the salt lakes are the long-abandoned missions of Abó, Quarai, and Gran Quivira. We pile out of the van and wander among the ruins of these huge red adobe buildings. The half walls wind into narrow paths, and it begins to feel as if I am wandering through a maze. Perhaps it is just that I have eaten nothing but trail mix. It is time for a significant amount of protein. However, this is not the road trip of my childhood. There are no bologna sandwiches, Lay's potato chips, or foil-wrapped Dr Pepper. We are part of the Pueblo Food Experience, and the food we eat today is all precontact.

We sit at picnic tables and begin to unwrap all the food we have brought. From Louie Hena there is a spinach wrap full of shredded turkey. From Marian Naranjo there are cold buffalo tamales. Roxanne has picked rosehips from the plants around the mission, and she adds this to the mix of food. All of it is tasty, and I begin to wonder if it is impolite to ask for thirds, perhaps even fourths. Well, if there's enough . . . why not?

The midday has turned into early afternoon. It is hotter than ever, yet clouds are beginning to form on the eastern horizon. It is not quite monsoon season, but we all know that this is the time when weather changes from second to second. Where before all was still, suddenly there is wind, rain, and hail. We're used to this. We expect it. So as we sit and eat, none of us is surprised that the wind has suddenly picked up speed. We hold tighter onto paper plates, try to keep plastic wrap from blowing off into the horizon. As always, I fumble in my pocket for a hair tie. I never remember to bring one. Undoubtedly, by the time this little windstorm is over, my hair will be a knot of tangles, and of course I have no comb or brush.

I'm completely preoccupied by the search for something to gather my hair into when the wind strengthens wildly and begins to whistle. In less than a few seconds, a dust devil has formed, and the significantly sized pillar of dust swirls through our picnic. Everyone falls silent. I know something has happened. Some energy was here, but I don't know how to say it.

On to the salt lakes.

When we get to the salt lakes, my eyes are burned by their white heat. I can feel the sun reflecting up onto the bottom of my chin. I should have worn shorts. My legs sweat and itch in my jeans.

The air smells like magnesium, but perhaps more important it just smells like mineral—like some fundamental element has been distilled down to its purest form. Something we need lives here. We crawl quickly through a broken section of barbed wire fence. This land belongs to someone, but no one knows whom, and I think perhaps it doesn't matter. Fences have always been a problem for us here in the US West. They are hostile creations.

So through the fence and on to the salt lake. I take off my hiking boots. The salt is so hot that it stings my feet. It is hotter than cement but more prickly and oddly soothing, like a hot-stone foot massage.

We all get to work. I don't know exactly how I am supposed to gather salt, but I figure it has to do with cracking and prying a few inches off the top crust. It comes off in flakes, mostly small (the size of a quarter or maybe a silver dollar), but sometimes it is huge, perhaps 3 to 4 inches in diameter. When that happens, it is like you have caught the biggest fish. We look at one another, show off, and brag: "Look it!" Chunks of raw salt are displayed everywhere.

I can't wait, and I don't think I need to wait. I want to know what raw salt tastes like. I crack off a nickel-sized piece of crust and put it in my mouth. It's salty, of course, but also earthy. I taste a hint of clay, but it is dry. Clay that has been cooked and has the texture of the dirt equivalent of beef jerky (or, in the case of our precontact diet, turkey/buffalo/venison/elk jerky). I could let these salt crusts melt on my tongue forever.

Roxanne has handed out freezer bags to each of us. We fill them with our crusts. Later, we will learn how to turn salt crust into salt that we can use on our food. But that is for when we are back amid the mountains and the Rio Grande. Now we sit in the middle of a desert that has no boundaries on an ancient salt lake that was once an ocean. We have followed an old path.

When I get home, it is almost dark. These are the longest days of the year, and we have been gone from sunup to sundown. It is so much colder in Chimayó. The barrancas that surround our house often keep the sun out of certain rooms, keeping them cool and comfortable in the summer heat, but right now I miss the white heat of the llano—the white heat of my childhood. I pick up my little freezer bag of raw salt. I go to wash the hours of gathered sweat from my face—my own personal salt, I think, as I pick up a bar of soap. I rinse my face with cold water, and when I look in the mirror, I find that tonight my skin is a much darker brown than it was when we started our southeastern migration at seven that morning.

COMMUNITY AND FOOD

Roxanne Swentzell

I HAVE BEEN FARMING FOR MANY YEARS, but the growing season of 2014 was memorable. This particular season was started like most others—preparing a field by tilling and making rows for irrigating. In another location, we planted in square waffled beds, which were flooded. Sometimes a plot was stone-mulched for dry-land farming. All are ways our ancestors grew their food.

This season, we had a number of interns and volunteers helping, six to nine of us at any given time—all women. The rows were made and planted, and the water flowed beautifully down each, soaking the dry, thirsty soil. We planted about an acre of corn, amaranth, beans, melons, chile, and cotton and a small patch of tobacco and peanuts. We waited for the water, sun, and soil to do their magic on the seeds. And then it happened!

It's always so exciting to watch the plants come up, pushing through that crust of earthskin to have a life in the sun. Gathering once a week to water and pull weeds, we came to do what women gathered together do best—gossip, share stories, cry, sing, and laugh. As the summer heat grew with the weeds, as spring sweaters were stripped off and long pants became shorter, clothing became a main topic. We admired one another's sense of fashion: tank tops, shorts, hats, sunglasses, sandals, boots, and hairstyles. Pulling a field of weeds by hand is hard work, but these women were not strangers to hard work. They knew humility and how to get something done, but they also knew how to have fun.

One of the ladies decided we should have theme days, during which we would dress up to work in the fields. The theme was decided the week before, to give us time to work up costumes. I remember one week looking up from the amaranth to find a fairy dressed in pink. Others had wings. Another week, I saw Amazon women in tough-looking poses wearing dinosaur earrings. Then there were the

Roxanne irrigating field, 2014 *(opposite)*

Flowering Tree interns pulling weeds, 2014

crowns for the queens of the weeds. Some towered high above the cornstalks and others were made of flowers and sticks, but the scene was unforgettable. People tend to think of farmers as men on tractors, but these farmers sat on the ground touching the soil inch by inch, noticing life up close while singing songs that came to mind. We laughed at ourselves in our ridiculous outfits, and got excited about dressing up for the next week. Now that's a different kind of farming!

After working hard mornings, we would stop for lunch, gathering in the shade of the porch and eating what someone had brought or ordered. We were tired but grateful for the time together, so much so that many times no one wanted to leave. At some point, one of the women thought we should add a writing part to this farming event. So for several weeks before lunch, we shared what we had written based on a theme we had decided on the week before. Some writings were poems; some fiction and some truths. Everyone was sad when the season came to an end and the gatherings stopped. We had other jobs and school to attend.

I can't help but think that a long time ago, when we were a tighter community, these kinds of gatherings happened every day, year-round, because that is how we survived and enjoyed life. We had to grow our own food because there were no stores. We cooked meals because there were no restaurants. During these times, we visited and saw one another often. We learned how to be respectful and grateful for our food because we knew all the steps it took to get it to our tables.

Emiliano and Freyer cleaning beans, 2014

In these modern times, it is rare to think of manual labor and farming as a good life. We hire someone else to do the work so that we don't have to. Is this because we have forgotten how to be communal? It is hard and lonely to work in a field without others to talk to and work alongside, so it is understandable that we have divorced ourselves from our food. But on a small part of the earth in the summer of 2014, there was a moment of remembering community and the blessings that come from being connected to one another and our food again. It was filled with laughter and care. It was filled with stories and imagination. It nurtured creativity and excitement. And, in the end, we not only had a truckload of corn, baskets of beans, and handfuls of chile. We had one another and the knowledge that having one another is everything.

A HUNTING STORY

Roxanne Swentzell

DURING OUR INITIAL TRIALS eating only our precontact Pueblo food, we decided as a group to go in on buying a whole buffalo to reduce our individual costs for buffalo meat. We found a German woman up in the Raton Mountains who had a herd and was willing to sell us one. So Marian and I took a trip north, driving through the mountains while telling stories of our lives. It was a hunting adventure for sure. The first thing we saw was a mountain sheep on the side of the road, then antelope close enough to make us both wish we had a bow and arrow. As we roamed dirt roads to find our buffalo herd, we stopped a few times to look at herds and to feel grateful for the honor of being able to choose our buffalo, our medicine, our food.

We found our ranch and the woman with the buffalo. She took us to the pens that held the grand animals we would choose from—dark, male buffalo with black horns and big manes. Marian and I had been in ceremony ever since starting up the truck, and wordlessly we smiled at each other, knowing that this was serious business. Now we three women stood before these mighty animals, feeling tiny but respectful while deciding who would live and who would feed us. We studied all of them, watching, waiting for a sign—something that would let us know which one. Maybe none would be given. As we watched, there was one buffalo who stared at us. I found myself scared to look back into his eyes, for his power was humbling. I kept averting my eyes but would find myself wandering back to him and his presence. Finally, without a doubt, we knew it was Number 14 (named for the tag on one ear). He would give us strength. He had very strong medicine. I soaked in his magnificence before he was led away.

Our new German friend gave us a place to spend the night. They would shoot Number 14 early in the morning so that we could take

Marian Naranjo and Roxanne with buffalo, 2014

him to the butcher before it got hot. That night we were quiet and thoughtful as we ate some buffalo tenderloin with a piñon and salt rub.

By the time we got down to the pens the next morning, Number 14 was dead. We took our cornmeal and prayed over him, thanking him and all who had brought us this blessing. They loaded Number 14 in the truck, and we followed them to the butcher in Raton. We told the butcher what cuts we wanted and tried to get every part of the animal we were allowed. The butcher gave us the hide and skull right off, and we started home. (The rest was packaged and delivered to us later.) We stopped along the way to walk our legs and look at our buffalo head. Number 14's eyes were open, but they stared off into nothing. Our conversations went to our prayers and our love for Pueblo culture. When we finished our prayers, I looked over: Number 14's eyes had closed. He had heard us.

We were blessed more at home as family met to throw cornmeal. Somehow we gained two turkeys that had just been shot that morning.

Overall, we two women felt pretty proud of our hunt. We passed out the meat (more than 500 pounds of it). Number 14 would feed many people for more than a year. I have had buffalo from different places and situations, but the meat from Number 14 was the best I have ever had.

I am still grateful for your strength, and from my mind's eye, I still see you walking and looking back at me, Number 14.

COMMUNITY FARMING

Roxanne Swentzell

AS A YOUNG CHILD, I would make small ditches with my hands to water the fruit trees and bushes in our front yard. Later, the excitement of growing pumpkins, tomatoes, and corn was something I looked forward to each spring. That excitement continues today.

Sometime in the mid-1980s, I became aware of seed saving and the differences between crop varieties and where they came from. My cultural roots became part of the understanding that plants, animals, and people are unique to their locations on this planet. Our traits evolved from environmental factors over many generations and years. Our DNA literally adjusted to such things as light, dryness, wetness, heat, cold, nutrients, and dangers. They all played a role in creating the amazing diversity of this planet.

We are at a new period in human history. We do not interact much with our food any longer and have lost sight of the community that generates it. Modern food production has become industrialized. Monocropping and eradicating species with herbicides and pesticides have become the norm. Whole ecosystems have been eliminated, weakening the basket of life to the point of real danger to all of us. We are losing the amazing diversity of this world. We used to be more rooted in place, taking time to notice the way a plant grew or where the sun came up each day. We could grow something from seed and be there to eat it too. It took much longer to travel from place to place, giving our bodies and minds time to adjust to new things. Some adjustments require remaining in the same environment for many generations. By this, I mean living in the natural environment of clouds, sunlight, dirt, water, air, animals, sounds, and wind, not just sitting in air-conditioned houses and cars. Our relationship to our environment is what makes us adjust to place. If we don't live within

Emiliano and Eleseo with harvest, 2013 *(opposite)*

Mary E. Dissette, *Woman hoeing in garden with two children, Nambe Pueblo, New Mexico*, ca. 1900 (NMHM/DCA 002999)

Emiliano and Eleseo helping Grandma Roxanne in garden, 2014 *(bottom)*

our natural world, we start disconnecting from it to the extent that our very survival is threatened.

When I realized our situation, I began to collect and grow out the traditional crops of the Pueblo people in an attempt to keep some of this diversity alive. Eventually, I had enough seed to build a seed bank here in Santa Clara Pueblo. I have been growing these seeds out every year since.

People have figured out many ways to grow crops. In much of the southwestern United States, we live in one of the harshest climates on earth. We get the hot, the cold, *and* the dry. Most areas receive only 5 to 10 inches of rain a year, and if temperatures aren't dropping below freezing, they are scorching above 100 degrees. This is the high desert. The Ancestral Pueblo people thrived in this region because they learned how to move within their environment sustainably. This took thinking in a communal sense. This took seeing themselves within the whole ecosystem, not as separate from it. As a Pueblo farmer, I've spent my life learning how to grow crops in this region, looking for signs of what works and what doesn't. It keeps me humble and has taught me a great respect for my ancestors' wisdom. Its keeps me watching and noticing all the things that make up the world around me. I am forever learning, forever praying, forever thankful, forever blessed.

A few years ago, I had the privilege of working with a group of young women over the summer in our field of corn, beans, squash, amaranth, and chile. Some were interns, some hired hands, some friends and family. We gathered once a week to lay out rows, plant, irrigate, weed, and then harvest our crop. It was very hard working in the hot sun, amid bugs, ants, and stickers, but we not only persevered; we had fun. I wondered many times why these ladies showed up week after week to struggle through these conditions and leave smiling. I realized it was about community. We gathered to gossip and share the week's events, to talk about boyfriends, girlfriends, struggles of one sort or another, to laugh and cry with one another, and in this way our sense of belonging increased. We usually moved through the field on hands and knees, pulling weeds and admiring

the corn growing stronger each week among insects, puppies, cats, and potsherds. Our intimate physical efforts with the ground, sky, and all that was between made us exist in a way that nothing else could. It was a whole community made up of clouds, water, plants, animals, insects, and people having conversations with one another on many levels.

The seeds in the ground pulled us to them and grew not only from sunshine and wet soil but also from human voices and human touch. We fed them, and in the end they fed us. Community is much larger than human. This is the story behind our return to eating our original food. It's about our relationship to place. In that field we again belonged to place, and everything felt better for it.

Santa Clara Blue Corn
(Flowering Tree garden, 2014)
(opposite)

A PATHWAY TO HEALTH

Annette M. Rodríguez

I JOINED THE PUEBLO FOOD EXPERIENCE months after most of the volunteers, on July 15, 2013. I finally joined after seeing the changes in energy and health of those around me and after taking a beautiful trip to ancestral salt beds to gather salt in June.

I have an extremely elevated immune system because of lupus, which I've struggled with for seventeen years. My specialists have prescribed steroids and chemotherapy since my diagnosis, and in 2011 I moved from once-a-week chemotherapy to daily chemotherapy after a biopsy showed major kidney damage. As I talked with the Pueblo Food Experience volunteers, some shared with me their lowering white blood counts and a reduction of inflammation as a result of the diet. I had considered joining the Pueblo Food Experience to reconnect with my ancestral foods and traditions—the project reminded me of my grandpa and his little milpa of corn and squash and how my mom told me about eating *verdolagas* (purslane), which is usually pulled out and thrown away like a weed. In addition to thinking about the foods that nourished my family in what is now northern Mexico and southern New Mexico, I started to think about a change in my diet as an important way to combat some of my lupus complications. After thinking about it for too long, I finally began the diet.

Immediately, I had strong cravings for butter and cheese. Then I had headaches and massive fatigue from giving up caffeine and sugar "cold turkey." The first two weeks I felt drained and tired. I avoided going inside the gas station because I was too tempted by the candy aisle and the smell of coffee. I also felt very emotional. I started to go through a grieving process when I realized that for the last couple of decades, I had no real sense of my own body. How much energy did I have on any given day? I didn't know, because so much of it was artificial, fueled by huge amounts of coffee and sugar. I felt sad

thinking about all my efforts in the last few years being based on artificial, bad fuel. I started feeling that so many things I had worked for had been poisoned by the energy produced from filling my body with refined sugars and caffeine. I cried more than once. I felt like a puppet controlled by these substances. I didn't even realize how addicted I had become to sugar and caffeine, and those first two weeks felt like a detox. I pushed through, but I felt exhausted and sad.

After week two, with the help of Pueblo Food Experience veterans, I moved away from the cravings and the sadness. I started to transition to natural sugars—lots of dried currants—and my coffee substitute, cacao. Coffee was a habit I had picked up very early in my life—maybe age six?—when I would brew and drink my dad's morning coffee. Giving up my daily coffee habit was very hard because it was as much about the ritual as it was about the effect. But cacao became my go-to beverage, along with cota tea and water, and after week two, I stopped craving coffee and sugary drinks.

I changed my daily habits totally—no eating out, no prepackaged foods. I had to plan carefully, making meals at home to carry with me to work, making Rox's special trail mix to have with me wherever I went. Before I knew it, I was past the detox and enjoying turkey and buffalo and elk. I harvested squash from our field and ate a feast every day. We noticed for the first time all the wild asparagus growing in and around our field. And we pulled wild onions, which taste so much better than store-bought. My first month of the Pueblo Food Experience was the best growing, cooking, and eating I'd ever done. I found I was totally conscious of everything I put into my body, which made it even more delicious. I savored every bite and every drink, and I stopped taking food for granted. For the first time ever, I realized how good summer squash is without butter and cheese.

More than anything, by week three, I was totally aware that our food is medicine and that in all my treatments for lupus I had ignored this. Even though I had tried to "eat healthy," most of the things I loved were inflammatories—butter, cheese, coffee, sugar, wheat bread—and had been making my condition worse. Within the first six weeks, I lost 17 pounds, mostly inflammation, and when I saw my mom, she got tears in her eyes and held my hand, pointing out that she'd never seen my fingers or knuckles without swelling. It's true—my rings were too big after the first month, and so were my clothes.

After the first month, I was constantly hiking up my jeans, and I had more energy than since I was a teenager. I woke up energized and rested instead of sore and still tired. Before the Pueblo Food Experience, getting out of bed every morning physically hurt from the arthritis and muscle pain that comes with lupus. I always had a hard time buttoning my shirts and tying my shoes, which is why years ago I started wearing pull-on boots. But within a month, the swelling and pain were gone; I was able to dress without discomfort since I had full use of my fingers, hands, and wrists; and I could work a full day without morning and afternoon coffee to get me through. I was able to take walks, stack wood, and keep up with everyone around me without resorting to a candy bar for a boost of energy. And yes, the swelling just kept going down. I also lost the lupus "butterfly rash" on my face that had marked me for years.

Removing the sugars, caffeine, starches, and processed foods from my diet immediately brought down my weight, my white blood cell count, and the inflammatory response they provoke. This is something all the prescribed medications hadn't been able to do. I feel better physically and emotionally. I feel solid in my body and connected to the land, water, and air that give me the food I eat. I feel more connected with the natural ways my grandparents planted, harvested, and cooked. My mom and aunts, who suffer from diabetes, high cholesterol, and autoimmune disorders, have all asked me for my secret. It's corn, beans, and squash. And plenty of buffalo and turkey and cota and cacao and piñons and pumpkin seeds and Marian's cookies! I am so grateful for the Pueblo Food Experience, which has taught me to honor my *antepasados* (ancestors) by honoring my own body. I feel I have more light and more energy to offer because of what has been offered to me. I won't go back to how I ate before. Thank you, Roxanne, and thank you, Pueblo Food Experience volunteers, for setting a path for me to walk.

The Recipes

IN CREATING THIS COOKBOOK, we aimed to maintain our traditional ways of understanding food and how it is consumed. We chose to begin our recipes with what we call the three sisters—corn, beans, and squash. The three sisters heal us and keep us balanced both physically and spiritually. They provide us with nutrition and connect us to the landscape of our ancestors.

We also chose to abide by our traditional ways of eating in how we organized our recipes. Our Pueblo ancestors were not confined by Western concepts such as breakfast, lunch, and dinner. To honor Pueblo foodways, we organize our recipes according to ingredient and/or use.

Many of the plants included in these recipes are indigenous to the southwestern United States; however, the majority of them can be found in grocery stores. Also, many of them, such as amaranth and purslane, are often mistaken for weeds. We hope this cookbook will open readers' eyes to the plants that surround them, and we hope that readers will recognize those plants as sources of nutrition.

All the recipes that follow were cooked and served at numerous potlucks held by Flowering Tree Permaculture Institute. (*Each recipe serves 6 or more.*) At those gatherings, we savored this food and enjoyed the company of those who created it. We hope you will do the same.

CORN AND GRAINS

MANY RECIPES IN THIS BOOK are based on corn and other grains. Because corn is the foundation of much of our food, it is important to distinguish the many forms of corn we use throughout this book:

Meal corn is matured non-sweet corn that has been dried. This corn comes in many colors. It is used to make masa and cornmeal.

Sweet corn has wrinkled kernels when it is dried. This corn is used for *chicos* and "green corn" recipes. It is also used to make roasted corn.

Dent corn has kernels that are literally dented. These kernels are used to make posole.

Along with corn, other grains are a vital part of our food culture. These include amaranth, quinoa, Indian rice grass seed, and lamb's quarters (purslane) seed. All of these small seeds can be ground into flour. They can then be added to any cornmeal to provide more nutritional value. Along with seeds, grains, and corn, dried nuts and fruits can also be ground into flour. Nut and fruit flour can be added to different foods to add protein or sweeten.

Nixtamal/Masa

Nixtamal is prepared corn that may be used in posole or ground into masa for tortillas and tamales.

2 gallons water
2 tablespoons lime (calcium hydroxide)
4 cups white corn

BOIL WATER in a stainless-steel pot. Carefully add lime to boiling water, stirring with a wooden spoon. Clean white corn and add to water. Continue to stir slowly. The corn will start to turn yellow. Turn the heat to a low boil. Stir occasionally (every 10 to 15 minutes). After 35 to 45 minutes, the solution will have completely separated the shiny cases of the corn. Once this casing is gone, place the corn into a colander and rinse with water for several minutes. Put the rinsed corn into the stainless-steel pot and add another gallon of water. Continue to stir the corn and then rinse again. After the second rinse, pour the corn back into the pot. Add more water until it covers the corn. Scrub the corn using only your hands. Repeat until the water washes clear.

Green Corn Tamales

1 dozen green corn* ears in husks
1 cup pure buffalo fat
1 1/2 teaspoons salt

*Green corn is corn that has not yet reached full maturity.

REMOVE THE CORN HUSKS and soak them in water until they are soft and pliable. Slice the corn kernels from the cobs. Blend the kernels until the mixture turns to mush. Blend buffalo fat and salt together. Add the mush and mix thoroughly. Place about 2 teaspoons of this mix onto each softened corn husk. Wrap each corn husk into a little bundle and tie it with a small strip of husk. Steam for 1 hour.

Tamales

This is a basic tamale recipe with a few alternatives. Other variations are included in this cookbook.

3 cups masa
1/2 teaspoon salt
Warm water (as needed)
2 dozen corn husks

MIX MASA AND SALT. Add warm water until the masa has a pancake consistency. Soak corn husks in warm water until they are soft and pliable. Place 4 to 5 tablespoons masa on each corn husk. Softly fold sides of husks around masa. Fold husk ends over and tie each tamale with a string of husk. Repeat until all masa is used. Place tamales in a steamer pot on the stove. Steam for at least 1 hour.

Alternatives

- Add flavor by mixing masa with meat broth instead of warm water.
- Add nuts, berries, squash, or meat on top of the masa spread on the corn husks. Fold and steam as usual. If you run out of masa, make more! (The same goes for other tamale recipes that follow.)
- Make sweet corn tamales by spitting into the masa mix and letting it stand overnight. Enzymes from your saliva will turn starches in the masa into sugars. (This is an ancient method that may not be used today. But some tamales that have been found at Ancestral Pueblo sites include evidence of this practice.) Wrap masa in husks and steam as usual. The masa will taste sweet.

Corn Tortillas

2 cups cornmeal
1 1/2 cups warm water
1/8 teaspoon salt

MIX ALL INGREDIENTS together until dough is no longer sticky. Form the dough into balls and flatten them by hand or with a tortilla press. Cook the flattened dough on a griddle until brown. Turn and repeat on the other side.

Roasted Corn

6 ears of fresh sweet corn, still in the husk

MAKE A FIRE and burn it down to the coals. Strip back the husk from each ear of corn but do not remove the husk completely. Remove all the silky hairs from the corn and then replace the husks onto the corn. Place ears on the hot coals. Let ears roast for 15 to 20 minutes, rotating them throughout.

Dried White Corn

White corn kernels (freshly sliced from an ear of corn)
Salted water

ROAST KERNELS in a cast-iron skillet on medium-high heat. Stir constantly. When kernels are a dark golden brown, add salted water to taste. Continue to stir until water evaporates. Lay out kernels on a towel to dry.

Blue Corn Cakes

Fat
1 cup blue cornmeal
1/4 cup quinoa flour
1/2 cup piñon nuts, shelled
1/2 cup currants
1 teaspoon salt
1 egg, beaten
1/4 cup sunflower oil
1/2 cup water

GREASE A LARGE MUFFIN PAN, using fat from any of the approved precontact animals (see Food List, p. 90). Preheat oven to 350 degrees. Stir together dry ingredients and then mix in the egg, sunflower oil, and water. Mix everything together until the dough is sticky. Divide the dough into 8 balls and pat them down with your fingers. Bake for 15 minutes or until cakes are solid in the middle. For best results, cool cakes before removing them from the baking pan.

Parched Corn

Cleaned white corn
3 tablespoons salt
2 cups water

HEAT A CAST-IRON DUTCH OVEN on medium heat. Add 2 cups white corn and stir. Continue to stir slowly so that the corn does not burn. The corn will begin to turn brown in about 8 to 10 minutes. It will also become shiny as it heats up. To make a brine, dissolve salt into water. Place brine in a shallow bowl or a spray bottle. If using a bowl, once the corn is parched, pour it into the brine solution. Quickly stir and then pour the corn into a strainer, separating the corn from the solution. Place brined corn on a flat pan to dry. If using a spray bottle, place the parched corn directly on the flat pan. Immediately spray the brine solution onto the parched corn. The heated corn will produce steam as the brine evaporates. Allow to dry.

Chicos

COOK CORN with salt for about 6 hours or in a crockpot overnight. Chicos can be served in a variety of dishes.

1 cup sweet corn (roasted)
6 cups water
1/2 teaspoon salt (amount may vary)

Atole

BOIL WATER in a saucepan. Place cornmeal in a cup and add a small amount of cold water, slowly mixing until there are no lumps. Slowly pour cornmeal into boiling water while stirring constantly. Add salt if desired. The mixture can also be made thicker and used as cereal.

2 cups boiled water
Cold water (as needed)
1/2 cup roasted cornmeal
Salt (to taste)

Buwah (Piki Bread)

The making of *buwah* is a community event. This recipe is constructed with the assumption that two or three women (culturally, it is women who make this bread) participate in the cooking.

- 1 tablespoon brains (from any approved precontact animal—see Food List, p. 90)
- 4 cups finely sifted cornmeal
- Up to 10 cups water
- 3 teaspoons ashes (preferably fourwing saltbush ashes and bean ashes)[1]

MASH BRAINS to the consistency of softened butter and set aside. Place cornmeal in a large mixing bowl and, with a wooden spoon, slowly add boiling water as needed. Stir constantly until the cornmeal batter is thick and completely smooth. Dissolve ashes in 2 cups of water. Slowly add ash water to batter until it reaches the consistency of thin pancake batter.

Heat a cooking stone using thinly chopped firewood.[2] When the stone is hot, use a cloth to grease the surface with a thin layer of brains. With a quick motion of your hand, spread a thin sheet of batter across the hot stone as evenly and quickly as possible. Most of the stone should be covered. When the batter starts to peel up, carefully lift the sheet and place it gently on a side pan. Repeat for a second sheet. As soon as the second sheet starts to peel up, gently lay the first sheet on top of it. Roll or fold both sheets together and place them on a side pan for eating. Repeat until all batter has been used.

1. Save the ashes from burning dried fourwing saltbush or bean plants.
2. Cooking stones are usually flat pieces of basalt varying from 1 to 2 inches thick and ranging from 1 to 2 feet long. They are usually passed down from generation to generation.

Harold Kellogg, *Making paper bread, San Ildefonso Pueblo, New Mexico, ca.* 1930 (NMHM/DCA 030946) *(opposite)*

Blue Corn Piñon Pancakes

IN A LARGE BOWL, sift together quinoa flour, cornmeal, baking powder, and salt. Form a well in the center and pour in the water, egg, and oil. Add piñon nuts and berries, then mix until smooth. Heat a lightly oiled griddle or frying pan over medium-high heat. Pour batter onto the griddle, using approximately 1/4 cup for each pancake. Turn when bubbles appear. Brown on both sides and serve hot. Top with berries and piñon nuts (as much as you like).

1/2 cup quinoa flour
1 cup blue cornmeal
3 1/2 teaspoons baking powder
1 teaspoon salt
1 1/4 cups water
1 egg
3 tablespoons sunflower oil
1 tablespoon berries, such as blueberries
1/4 cup piñon nuts, shelled
Berries and shelled piñon nuts for topping (optional)

Blue Cornballs

MIX CHAMISA or bean ash with 4 tablespoons boiling water and set aside. Mix cornmeal and the rest of the boiling water. Pour the ash water mix through a strainer into the dough. This will turn the dough blue. Shape the dough into small balls and drop into boiling water for 10 minutes. (Larger balls can be made into dumplings.) Once cooked, blue cornballs can be eaten as is or added to stews.

2 teaspoons chamisa or bean ash (the burned residue of dried bean pods)
8 tablespoons boiling water
1/2 cup blue cornmeal

Indian Rice Flour

WHEN THE RICE IS RIPE, clean the rice seeds from their hulls. Toast the seeds in a pan on low heat. Grind into a flour or meal.

Native wild rice

Popped Amaranth

HEAT A FRYING PAN on high. Place a handful of amaranth grain into the heated pan while stirring constantly. If the pan has reached the correct temperature, the amaranth will pop like popcorn. After it has popped, remove immediately and place in a bowl. It is ready to eat.

1/2 cup amaranth grain

Roxanne cleaning amaranth seed, 2014 *(opposite)*

BEANS

Crockpot or Stovetop Beans

Crockpot or stovetop beans are a nutritious staple of the PFE diet that can be a main dish or a side dish to complement many meals.

2 cups pinto beans
6 cups water
2 teaspoons salt (or as needed)

Crockpot:

COMBINE BEANS, water, and salt in a crockpot. Put on high heat and cook for 6 to 8 hours. Stir occasionally and add water as needed. Beans are done when they are soft. Salt to taste.

Stovetop:

SOAK BEANS IN WATER overnight. Then add salt and simmer on the stove for 6 to 8 hours. Stir occasionally and add water as needed. Salt to taste.

Bean Snack

2 cups fully cooked beans (cooked overnight in a crockpot)

STRAIN WATER FROM BEANS. Lay out beans on a cookie sheet and slowly dry them in an oven at 225 degrees. Stir occasionally until beans are totally dried out. The beans can be eaten as a snack. You can also rehydrate them at a later date to make soups or refried beans.

Bean Flour

2 cups dried refried beans

GRIND DRIED BEANS on a metate or in a meal grinder until they have the consistency of flour. This flour can be used in other recipes, such as cake and cookie recipes.

Santa Clara Bean Loaf

1/2 onion
1 large tomatillo
4 cups cooked mashed beans
1/2 cup crumbly corn masa
1/2 cup sunflower seeds
1 turkey egg
1 teaspoon salt

MINCE ONION THOROUGHLY. Chop tomatillo into cubes. Mix all ingredients together. Once they are thoroughly mixed, pack them into a loaf pan. Bake at 350 degrees for 45 minutes.

SQUASH

Baked Squash

CUT SQUASH IN HALVES. Scrape out seeds and pulp. (Save seeds. These can be roasted and eaten as snacks or used as a base for oil.) Salt squash halves and place in the oven. Bake in oven at 350 degrees until squash is soft (about 1 hour). To add flavor, add currants and piñon nuts before baking squash. Salt to taste.

1 winter squash
1/8 teaspoon salt
Currants and shelled piñon nuts (optional)

Squash Chips

CUT SQUASH INTO THIN SLICES and place on a drying rack. Add salt if desired. Allow to dry until crispy. Slices can be eaten like chips.

2 summer squashes
Dash of salt (optional)

Butternut Squash Soup

1 butternut squash
Water
3 cups turkey broth
Salt (to taste)

CUT SQUASH INTO HALVES or quarters. Clean seeds out of squash. Place in a baking dish with about 1 inch of water. Bake squash at 375 degrees for 1 hour. When squash is soft, place it in a blender. Add turkey broth until it covers the pieces of squash in the blender. Blend thoroughly. Pour the mixture into a stockpot and simmer for 1 hour. When it is done, add salt as needed.

Corn Squash Pudding

2 cups white corn
1 zucchini
2 tablespoons sunflower seeds or piñon nuts, shelled

CUT CORN KERNELS FROM THE COB. Finely dice the zucchini. Chop the sunflower seeds or pine nuts extremely fine. Mash all ingredients together until the texture is milky. (A blender helps.) Bring the mixture to a boil and simmer until it is thick like pudding.

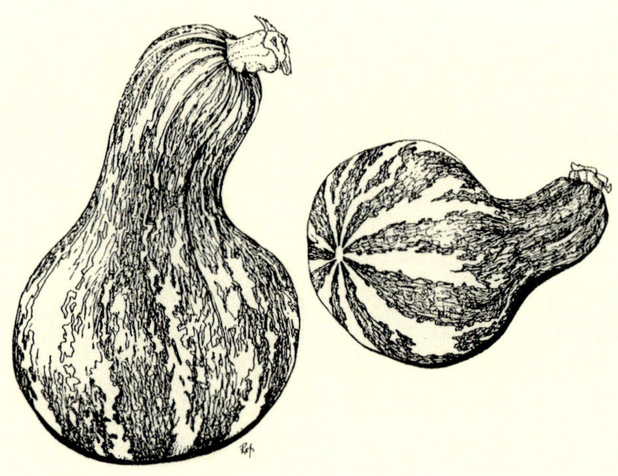

PROTEINS

Buffalo Roast

You may use rump, chuck/shoulder, or round steak. Browning the roast well in a cast-iron pan adds iron to the meat and also keeps moisture from escaping while cooking.

- 1 tablespoon sunflower oil
- 2 to 3 pound buffalo roast
- 1/2 cup water
- 1/4 cup chopped wild onions
- Several sage leaves
- Buffalo stock (if needed)

ADD SUNFLOWER OIL to a large cast-iron pan on medium to high heat. When oil is hot and almost smoking, brown roast on all sides (a good set of metal tongs is helpful). Brown 2 minutes on each side for a total of about 10 minutes. Watch carefully. Set the pan aside. (Don't wash it yet!)

Preheat oven to 275 degrees. Put water into the browning pan and bring to a boil. Pour buffalo water and any pan scrapings into a roasting dish. Add chopped wild onions and sage leaves. Put browned roast into roasting dish. Liquid should rise to about 1 inch; add buffalo stock (especially the fatty top of the stock) if needed.

Roast covered for two and a half hours. Then turn the roast. Be sure to bring wild onions and liquid to top of the roast. Roast until the meat is tender and falls away with a fork. This varies based on cut of the roast. Keep in mind that buffalo has a much lower fat content than beef or pork, so roast may take shorter time than you are used to. When you turn the roast, you may want to add more stock (especially the fatty top).

When the roast is done, remove cover and caramelize the top with the dry heat of the oven. Once the roast has a nice brown top, remove from heat and from the baking dish. Rest the meat (cover with tin foil to keep more moisture in) for at least 10 minutes to allow the juices to stay sealed in.

Season with raw salt and eat with your hands! Or eat in a corn tortilla.

Buffalo Tongue

1 buffalo tongue
Water (as needed)
2 teaspoons salt

PLACE TONGUE in a saucepan large enough to contain it. Fill saucepan with water until tongue is completely covered. Add salt. Bring to a boil on high heat. Cover pan and reduce heat to a low boil. Cook for 3 to 4 hours, until a fork can easily penetrate the outer layer of the tongue. Remove from heat and strain out water.

Buffalo Meatballs and Quinoa

1 cup quinoa
2 pounds ground buffalo meat
1 cup finely chopped mushrooms
1/2 teaspoon salt
2 turkey eggs (or duck eggs), beaten
Water (as needed)

STEAM QUINOA AND SET IT ASIDE. Mix ground buffalo with mushrooms, salt, and eggs. Boil water in a large saucepan. Form ground buffalo mixture into meatballs and place in the boiling water. Cover and cook until meatballs are done. Mix quinoa and meatballs before serving.

Elk Meatballs

ROLL ELK MEAT INTO BALLS. Cut zucchini into slices and place in a saucepan with about 1 cup water. Add corn kernels. Add meatballs and salt. Cover and let steam for 40 minutes or until meat is cooked.

1 pound ground elk meat
1 zucchini
Water (as needed)
1 cup sweet corn kernels
1/2 teaspoon salt

Elk Casserole

PREHEAT OVEN TO 350 DEGREES. Chop wild onions or garlic chives. Stew tomatillos. Mix all ingredients together. Place in a bread loaf pan and cover. Bake for 1 hour.

1/2 cup wild onions or garlic chives
1 1/2 cups tomatillos
2 pounds ground elk
2 turkey eggs
1 1/2 teaspoons salt
1/4 cup amaranth or quinoa

Buffalo Tamales

2 small zucchinis
1 pound ground buffalo
Dash of salt, plus 1/3 teaspoon
1 cup corn masa
Warm water (as needed)
2 dozen corn husks

IN SAUCEPAN, cook diced zucchini and buffalo until well cooked. Add water if it is too dry. Salt to taste and set aside. Pour water in a steamer pan and place on hot stove. Place corn masa in medium-size bowl. Add 1/3 teaspoon salt. Slowly add warm water until masa is the consistency of pancake batter.

Soak corn husks in warm water until soft. Take one husk and place about 1 tablespoon of masa in center. Spread out. Place 1 heaping teaspoon of buffalo/zucchini mix in center of masa on corn husk. Roll corn husk, fold ends, and tie lightly with strips of corn husk. Place in steamer. Repeat until all masa is used. Cover steamer and let cook for one hour.

Turkey Tamales

2 dozen corn husks
4 cups masa
4 cups turkey broth
1/2 teaspoon salt
Roasted turkey leftovers (everything except bones)
Water (as needed)

SOAK AND SOFTEN the corn husks. Mix masa with turkey broth instead of water. Add salt to mixture to make dough. Wrap about 1 tablespoon masa and 1 heaping teaspoon turkey inside each corn husk. Tie husks with strips of softened husk. Steam for 1 1/2 hours. Tamales may be eaten hot or cold.

Turkey Tomatillo Tamales

DICE TOMATILLOS into small pieces. Shred turkey meat into small pieces. Add tomatillos to shredded turkey. Add salt and stir well. Mix water and grease into the corn masa until it feels and looks like dough. If it needs more moisture, add water. Soak corn husks in water until they are soft and malleable. Place about 1 tablespoon corn masa onto each corn husk and flatten masa in the center. Add about 1 heaping teaspoon turkey/tomatillo mix to the middle of the masa and roll up each husk. Tie the ends of the corn husks, but not too tightly. Steam tamales for at least 1 hour.

4 tomatillos
1 pound boiled turkey meat
1/2 teaspoon salt
2 1/2 cups masa
Water (as needed)
Turkey fat and grease
2 dozen corn husks

Juniper Lamb Stew

CUT LAMB into small cubes. Slice kernels from ears of corn. Chop the zucchinis. Crush the dried juniper berries. Mix all ingredients in a large sauce pan. Add water, cover the pan with its lid, and simmer for 1 hour.

2 pounds lamb
6 ears corn
2 zucchinis
5 dried juniper berries
6 wild spring onions
1 1/2 tablespoons salt
4 cups water

Sheep Corn Soup

DICE MEAT. Simmer in water until tender. Add corn kernels and salt.

2 cups lamb
6 cups water
Kernels from 8 ears corn
1 teaspoon salt

Jackrabbit Stew

1 jackrabbit
5 wild spring onions
3/4 cup grease or fat
1 teaspoon salt
2 quarts water
2 cups cooked posole

CUT JACKRABBIT INTO CUBES. Chop wild spring onions and sauté them in a pan with the grease or fat. When onions have browned a little, add them to the rest of the ingredients. Simmer everything in a stockpot for 2 hours.

Rabbit Stew

1 rabbit
1 cup dried beans
3/4 cup chicos
Salt (to taste)

BUTCHER AND CLEAN RABBIT. Place all ingredients in a crock-pot. Add enough water to cover ingredients. Cook on medium heat overnight.

Goose

Hornos and *buntes* (outdoor ovens) are great for cooking meats. You can also cook meats in the ground by digging a hole and making a hot fire. The fire will heat the walls of the hole, which will radiate heat back to cook your food.

1 goose

HEAT A BUNTE until the walls are white. Place goose on a tray. Cover it with a clay lid or aluminum foil. Close the oven well. Let the goose cook for most of the day or overnight.

Stuffed Dove (or Quail)

CLEAN BIRD, removing feathers and insides. Boil spinach twice, straining the water each time in order to take out bitterness. Mix piñons, salt, and *tsimaha* together and stuff inside cavity of bird. Bake in oven at 375 degrees for about 30 minutes or until done.

4 doves or quail
1 cup cooked wild spinach
1/3 cup piñon nuts, shelled
1/2 teaspoon salt
1/2 cup tsimaha (fresh wild parsley), chopped

Turkey Corn Dogs

MIX MASA, EGGS, and salt together with warm water. The mixture should be neither too wet nor too dry. Wrap the masa around the turkey dogs. Cover them and bake at 350 degrees for 20 minutes or steam them in a steamer until the masa is thoroughly cooked.

2 cups masa
2 turkey eggs, beaten
1 1/2 teaspoons salt
Warm water (as needed)
1 package turkey hot dogs

Turkey-Wrapped Asparagus with Piñons

12 thick turkey slices
12 asparagus stalks
1/2 cup piñon nuts, shelled and crushed
Water (as needed)

WRAP TURKEY SLICES around the asparagus. Sprinkle with piñon nuts. Bake in a covered dish at 350 degrees for 45 minutes. Add water to keep the dish from becoming overly dry.

Piñon Trout

1/8 cup piñon nuts, shelled
1/8 teaspoon salt
1 trout

SMASH PIÑONS INTO CRUMBS. Add salt. Rub piñon/salt crumb mixture all around the trout. Leave any excess mixture on top of the trout. Cook in oven at 350 degrees until done, about 20 to 30 minutes.

Baked Blue Cornmeal Catfish

1/2 cup blue cornmeal
1 tablespoon salt
1 tablespoon garlic powder
2 eggs
1 fillet of catfish
Duck or turkey fat

IN A MEDIUM BOWL, mix cornmeal, salt, and garlic powder. Mix in eggs to create a batter. Dip catfish fillet into batter, covering it entirely. Grease a baking dish or sheet with duck or turkey fat. Bake catfish at 375 degrees for 25 minutes.

Wild Spinach Tomatillo Omelet

CHOP TOMATILLO into small slices. Chop spinach into small slices. Beat turkey eggs and add all ingredients together. Cook in a saucepan and stir constantly until done. Add salt to taste.

1 large tomatillo
1/2 cup wild spinach
2 turkey eggs
Salt

Prickly Pear Eggs

1 pad from prickly pear cactus
1 tablespoon sunflower oil
2 eggs
Salt

AFTER REMOVING THE THORNS, slice or dice the prickly pear pad. Place sunflower oil into a pan over medium heat. Add the pad and sauté until soft. Scramble the eggs in a separate bowl and add eggs to the pan. Mix together until eggs are thoroughly cooked. Salt to taste.

Fried Grasshoppers

1/2 cup oil or melted animal fat
Grasshoppers*
Salt

HEAT OIL OR FAT in a deep frying pan. To make sure the pan has reached the proper temperature, toss in a live grasshopper, which should immediately sizzle. If the grasshopper does not sizzle, the pan is not hot enough. Do not torture grasshoppers by putting them on a pan that is not yet hot enough. When grasshoppers turn orange-pink, they are done. Scoop them out with a strainer. Place on paper towel or cloth to soak up excess grease. Salt to taste. Eat grasshoppers whole.

*To catch grasshoppers, go outside early in the morning when it is still cool. Grasshoppers are slow when they are cold. Place them in a lidded jar. Grasshoppers can be stored in the refrigerator until ready to cook.

Rox

GREENS

Prickly Pear Pads

CUT PADS from a cactus plant. Singe the thorns until they can be scraped from the pads. Cook the pads in boiling water.

Prickly pear pads (as many as you would like to eat)
Water (enough to cover pads)

Dandelion Greens

Wild dandelion greens must be gathered in early spring. Once they flower, the leaves taste bitter, but the flowers can still be eaten whole.

EAT GREENS FRESH in a salad in early spring or boil greens to create a warm vegetable side dish.

Wild dandelion greens (as many as you would like to eat)

Purslane

PURSLANE (also known as verdolagas), a plant native to Pueblo landscapes, can be eaten fresh as a snack or as part of a salad. It can also be cooked and served as a warm vegetable side dish. Another option is purslane cooked with eggs.

Purslane (as much as you would like to eat)

Three-Sister Salad

1/2 cup white corn from 2 cobs
1/4 cup prickly pear pads
1/2 cup yellow squash
1/2 cup black beans
1/2 cup squawbush berry water*
Salt

BOIL CORN UNTIL TENDER. Let corn cool before removing kernels from the cob. Place kernels in a large mixing bowl. Rinse prepared (thorns removed) prickly pear pads. Dice them into cubes. Dice squash into cubes as well. Place squash and prickly pear pads into a hot frying pan and lightly sauté them. Once they are sautéed, add them to the mixing bowl with the corn. Cook the black beans. Put beans, corn, squash, and prickly pear pads into the large mixing bowl. Add squawbush berry water. Salt as needed.

*Place ripe berries in water, shake them, and drain out the water.

Rocky Mountain Bee Weed

Another native plant of Pueblo landscapes, it must be collected while still young or it will taste bitter.

Rocky Mountain bee weed (as much as you want to eat)
Water (enough to cover bee weed)

PREPARE ROCKY MOUNTAIN BEE WEED by boiling it. Serve it warm as a vegetable side dish.

Salad Ingredients

FRESH SALAD can be made by gathering various wild and cultivated greens. The following are some of the greens we found were good for salads. Wild greens tend to be stronger tasting than cultivated greens. We suggest tasting the greens first, then combining a couple of each type (wild and cultivated).

Amaranth sprouts
Cattail shoots
Dandelions
Mint
Piñon nuts
Purslane
Squash blossoms
Sunflower seeds and sprouts
Tomatillos
Wild onions
Wild spinach (lamb's quarters)

Salad Dressings

BECAUSE WILD GREENS are so tasty, we found that they don't need dressing. But if you do want to add a little sweetness, try the following dressings. When berries are in season they're readily available. Just gather a few handfuls, mash up berries, and mix with a tablespoon or two of water until you get the desired consistency.

Currant mush
Plum mush
Raspberry mush
Serviceberry mush
Squawbush berry mush

DRINKS

Sunflower Coffee

BROWN HULLS in a skillet. Stir frequently to keep hulls from burning. Once hulls are browned, grind them fine. Steep ground hulls in boiling water for 3 minutes.

- 2 teaspoons sunflower seed hulls
- Boiling water (as needed)

Squawbush Lemonade

Squawbush (scientific name *Rhus trilobata*) berries should be gathered in September before they dry out. Tea from the boiled berries tastes like lemonade, hence the recipe name.

TIE SQUAWBUSH BERRIES into a porous cloth. Boil berries inside the cloth in water for 15 minutes. Mash the berries, add water as necessary, and drink. Serve hot or cold.

- 1/2 cup ripe squawbush berries (as many as you want)
- 1 quart water

Berry-Veggie Smoothie

5 organic strawberries
4 stems raw organic asparagus
Handful of blueberries
3 pitted prunes
1 cup water

PLACE ALL FRUITS and vegetables into a blender. If you would like, add ice. Blend thoroughly.

Mint Tea

Fresh mint leaves (as much as you want)
Water

ADD MINT LEAVES to water in a large sun tea jar. Leave outside in the sun for several hours. Serve hot or cold.

Cota Tea

Cota is native to the Pueblo landscape. Harvest the plant by cutting off its leaves and yellow flowers.

BOIL COTA in water for 5 to 10 minutes to make tea.

Cota (as much as you like), either dried or fresh
6 cups water

Prickly Pear Fruit Juice

SLICE OPEN FRUIT. Allow it to dry completely. Grind dried fruit very fine on a stone or with a coffee grinder. Sift out the seeds and save the powder. Pair 1 teaspoon powder to 1 cup water to make juice.

Prickly pear fruit, ripe
Water (as needed)

DESSERTS

Grandma Marian's Cookies

PREHEAT OVEN TO 350 DEGREES. Boil cacao powder or niblets in water. After boiling, strain out the cacao. Place currants or strawberries in the liquid and boil lightly until they have softened. Mix together cornmeal flour and nuts or seeds. Add this to the cacao liquid mixture. The consistency should be like that of cookie dough. Place spoonfuls of the mixture onto a baking sheet. Bake for 30 minutes.

- 1/2 cup cacao powder or niblets
- 1 1/2 cups water
- 1/2 cup currants or dried strawberries
- 1 cup cornmeal flour (white, blue, or yellow)
- 1 cup piñon nuts, shelled (or pumpkin or sunflower seeds)

Blueberry Cake

PREHEAT OVEN TO 350 DEGREES. Boil plums in water. Once plums have softened, mash them. You can also blend the plums until their texture is like a watery pudding. Add corn masa, flour, and eggs to the mash. Mix extremely well. If the mixture is too dry, add water. Add blueberries and softly stir them in with a spoon. Place mixture into a greased cake pan. (Grease can be made from animal fat or shelled piñon nuts or sunflower seeds.) Bake for 40 minutes.

- 1 cup plums, dried and pitted
- 1 cup water
- 2 cups corn masa
- 1 cup bean flour (or garbanzo bean flour)
- 2 eggs
- 1 cup blueberries

Chocolate Cake

PLACE PLUMS OR PRUNES in a saucepan. Add water. Heat until the plums are well cooked or the prunes are rehydrated. Mash into a thick syrup (about 2 cups). Add more water if needed. In a large bowl, mix masa, bean flour, and cocoa flour with the plum mush. Add two turkey eggs and continue to mix. If mixture is too thick for cake batter, add water. Pour batter into two small cake pans greased with piñon nuts. Cook at 350 degrees for 30 minutes or until done. Cool and top with remaining plum mush. Decorate cake with as many mint leaves and raspberries as you like.

- 2 cups plums (pitted) or prunes
- 1/2 cup water
- 3/4 cup masa
- 1 cup bean flour
- 1/2 cup cocoa flour
- 2 turkey eggs, beaten
- 1/2 cup piñon nuts, shelled and crushed
- Mint leaves and raspberries (optional)

Cocoa Piñon Cake

PREHEAT OVEN TO 350 DEGREES. Add masa, bean flour, cocoa flour, and eggs to plum mash. Mix extremely well. If the mixture is too dry, add water. Add piñon nuts and softly stir them in with a spoon. Place the mixture into a greased cake pan. (Grease can be made from animal fat, piñon nuts, or sunflower seeds.) Bake for 40 minutes.

- 2 cups masa
- 1/2 cup bean flour
- 1/2 cup cocoa flour
- 2 eggs
- 1 cup plum mash (see recipe above)
- 1/2 cup piñon nuts, shelled

Currant Pie

- 1 1/2 cups corn masa
- 1/2 cup amaranth flour
- 1 1/3 teaspoons salt
- 2 eggs
- 1/2 cup plums (dried and pitted)
- Water (as needed)
- 2 cups currants

PREHEAT OVEN TO 350 DEGREES. Mix masa and amaranth flour together. Add salt and eggs to the flour mixture. Press mixture into a pie pan to make crust. Boil plums down with water until they become a syrup. Mix currents and syrup and spread them over the pie crust. Bake in the oven for 40 minutes.

Pumpkin or Squash Pie

BOIL PUMPKIN OR SQUASH until soft. Scoop flesh into a bowl. Add 2 eggs and plum mush. Mix well and set aside. Mix amaranth flour, masa, 1 egg, salt, and water until dough is as workable as pie crust. Roll into a ball, press out in a tortilla press (or by hand), and place in a pie pan. Pour in squash filling and place in a heated oven. Bake at 350 degrees for 45 minutes.

1 pumpkin or squash
3 turkey or duck eggs
1/2 cup plum mush
1 cup amaranth flour
1/2 cup corn masa
1/2 teaspoon salt
Water (as needed)

Banana Yucca

The ripe fruit of this plant (scientific name *Yucca baccata*) is sweet and soft like a banana, hence its common name, banana yucca.

YUCCAS SEND UP A SHOOT high above the plant. Flowers grow along the shoot and when the flowers are pollinated, fruits that look like short fat bananas form. The fruit starts out green and hard, then turns yellow or tan and becomes soft when ripe in late summer or early fall. Eat fruit right after harvesting.

Banana yucca (as much as you want to eat)

SNACKS AND CONDIMENTS

Trail Mix

MAKE SURE ALL NUTS AND SEEDS are properly shelled. Place nuts and seeds in a saucepan and toast lightly over medium heat for 2 to 3 minutes, stirring constantly. In a large bowl, combine all ingredients. Stir well.

1 cup piñon nuts
1 cup pumpkin seeds
1 cup sunflower seeds
1 cup dried currants
1 teaspoon salt

Popcorn

PLACE POPCORN IN A SAUCEPAN. Cover pan and constantly move it over high heat until all kernels are popped. (Oil is not needed.) Salt to taste.

1/3 cup popcorn
Salt

Roasted Piñon Nuts

Collect piñons in the fall, when pinecones start opening. Place a sheet or tarp under a pine tree and shake its branches, or just gather piñon nuts from the ground. Choose the dark brown ones. The light ones are empty and do not contain nuts. Piñons can be eaten raw or roasted. The roasted ones can be stored longer and can be saved for winter.

PLACE A LAYER OF NUTS on a flat pan. Place in a hot oven. Roast at 375 degrees for 10 to 20 minutes, stirring often. Check if the nuts are ready by eating one. The flavor will have changed, but the nut will not taste burned. Lay out nuts on a wet cloth, roll them, and sprinkle them with salt to taste.

Piñon nuts
Salt

Jerky

USING A SHARP KNIFE, cut meat into thin flat slices. Lightly salt both sides of meat. Hang pieces of meat on string or wire, away from moisture and flies. Let dry until crispy.

Boneless meat of elk, deer, antelope, fish, or birds
Salt

Pueblo Crackers

GRIND NUTS AND SEEDS together. Add salt. Form mixture into small balls. Flatten balls into thin wafers. Wrap each ball in a softened corn husk. Bake at 350 degrees for 40 minutes.

1/2 cup piñon nuts, shelled
1/2 cup sunflower seeds, shelled
1/4 teaspoon salt
4 corn husks

Turkey Spread

2 cups finely chopped cooked turkey
1 cup finely chopped tomatillos
1/2 teaspoon salt

MIX INGREDIENTS and eat as a dip or spread on tortillas or Pueblo Crackers.

Piñon Butter

2 cups piñon nuts, shelled
Salt

CRUSH NUTS until creamy. Add salt to taste.

Marrowbone Butter

2 or 3 shinbones (from any approved precontact animal—see Food List, p. 90)
Salt

CRACK BONES and roast at 350 degrees for 1 hour or until marrow is soft. Scoop out marrow and serve on tortillas. Add salt to taste.

Piñon Gravy

CRUSH NUTS. Boil them until oil rises to the top. Skim the oil and boil the nuts again. Season gravy with salt to taste.

2 cups piñon nuts, shelled
4 cups water
Salt

Fourwing Saltbush

This plant is native to Pueblo landscapes. It is called saltbush because its leaves have a salty flavor.

BURN THE PLANT and collect the ashes. Use them as a substitute for salt or baking soda.

Fourwing saltbush (as much as you want)

Salt

Salt can be found in old salt beds, where it will resemble a crust. The air will smell of magnesium.

COLLECT THE TOP CRUST from a salt bed. Soak the crust in water overnight. In the morning, strain off the clear top water and discard the muddy mixture at the bottom of the pail. Pour the clear salty water into pans and allow the water to evaporate. You can speed up this process by placing the pans in an oven on low heat. When all the water has evaporated, you are left with salt.

Raw salt

THE FOOD LIST

Gathered Foods

Asparagus
Blueberries
Cactus pads and fruit
Chokecherries
Cota
Currants
Dandelions
Fourwing saltbush
Indian rice grass
Juniper
Mint
Mushrooms
Osha (wild celery) root
Piñon (pine) nuts
Purslane
Raspberries
Rosehips
Sage
Serviceberries
Squawbush berries
Watercress
Wild grapes
Wild onions
Wild parsley
Wild plums
Wild spinach
Wild strawberries
Willow bark

Hunted Foods and Proteins

Antelope

Buffalo

Deer

Duck and duck eggs

Eel (which once swam up the Rio Grande from the Gulf of Mexico)

Elk

Fish

Geese and geese eggs

Grasshoppers

Grubs

Mountain sheep

Pack rats

Pheasant, doves, and other regional birds

Prairie dogs

Quail and quail eggs

Rabbits

Squirrels

Turkey and turkey eggs

Cultivated Foods

Amaranth

Beans

Corn (non-GMO)

Squash and squash seeds

Sunchokes

Sunflowers

Tomatillos

THE SPIRIT OF FOOD

Marian Naranjo

MY FIRST MEMORY OF FOOD involves our traditional foods, because my mother and father were both farmers. They were very connected with the food they grew up with. And because of their connection to their diet, it also became our family diet. We often made *ah-geh* with *sakawe* (atole with milk). I remember eating this as a baby. I remember the smells and the taste. How ah-geh made me feel—a tingly sensation when I felt the warmth of the food. It was really a good feeling, and watching my mother prepare it was an important part of the feeling. The way she did it, I know that love went into it.

When I got older, I realized that this food was the same food my parents had eaten when they were growing up. Then, as I got more knowledgeable, I realized that this was the same food our ancestors ate. I can imagine back in the day when our ancestors ate or drank that atole. It was a food that stimulated us—filled us with vitality. I have seen people on their deathbeds who could not eat hospital food. But when they were given atole, they ate it like it was going out of style. It was an honor to witness that connection.

Now, with all the corporations in the United States, with all the fast foods, it is different. Eat this. Buy this. The emphasis is on right now instead of the whole process—the whole process of growing, of not wanting anything to go to waste because it took a lot of work to get the food to the edible stage. The process of community—everybody had a position concerning the food, and the work wasn't hard because everyone participated. That has changed.

When I was growing up, my relatives were farmers. We still had that communal connection, and my brothers would grow the food. We, the younger ones, would shuck. My mother would store the food. But now things are so fast-paced. Now time in a day goes so quickly. That whole communal thing is not paid attention to, unless you're

Edward S. Curtis, *In the Grey Morning, San Ildefonso Pueblo, New Mexico,* 1905 (NMHM/DCA 144547) (*opposite*)

consciously connected to it. This project, the Pueblo Food Experience, has brought consciousness and awareness back to those communal connections.

Before beginning the Pueblo diet, I was headed for a stroke. I weighed more than 200 pounds. I was not centered totally in my own being. I was becoming an elder, and I had a second chance. I call it a second chance because when you have grandchildren, things are different. They gave me a second chance. My own children were like my guinea pigs. I didn't know it then, but they were. I raised four children by myself, and we weren't rich, so a lot of our food had to be made from scratch. That was the cheapest way, and I had more time than money. That was a good thing. Because of that, they were brought up in the same manner as I had been.

Before beginning the Pueblo diet, I really wanted transformation for myself. When this diet came along, it came at a perfect time. My spiritual grounding was ready for a deeper transition. Many things happened at the same time for me, and it made for a beautiful experience. I became more connected with my village and more aligned within myself, so not only was there weight loss, but there was also more energy. During the three years I participated in the diet, I tried to stay focused because it felt so good. I became more connected, to the point where I was able to incorporate this connection into my work and other activities, which was a gift.

As a founder and director of an organization called Honor Our Pueblo Existence, I found this connection extremely important. For many years, we have worked on improving the environment—air, water, and land—because our teaching is that if we don't take care of the environment, it's not going to take care of us. We began to connect more with our acequia and get more involved with our seeds, our food. We brought awareness to people who wanted to join with us and organize. We realized what our future needs looked like. Our air, water, and land are not being taken care of. The work became very personal. Doing cultural preservation work is another aspect of our organization, so we're kind of going back into our history.

We built ten buntes for the women in the families to make bread in abundance. Of course, they were also used for roasting corn and even just cooking in a big way to provide for many people. We started there and then took it farther down through our history to develop what we call buwah, our ancestors' first bread, made with blue corn and batter and cooked on stones. Food has spiritually connected us. We are teaching other women how to cook this way. It's a process of bringing back traditions that have not been practiced since the 1920s. We are listening to the stories of our elders, about what they remember from when they were little. And how they remember watching the women make buwah on stones. Then the practice disappeared because the railroad came. Then came these other methods of cooking, and then there was money and all of that.

So now that I am an elder, I wish I would have started this diet full-heartedly when I was younger. I now have bone problems, and maybe if I had followed this diet earlier, I would not be in this situation now. The rest of me is so energized and excited to continue doing the work. I love being cautious and conscious. I love that the grandchildren come here and it's an exciting adventure for them. They're growing up with fast food, and then they come to Grandma's and it's this whole other thing. I love watching their little faces because they're such little sponges, eager and open to hear old stories. How come this food? The work is so personal because it's work I do in my household—my household is my office. It's the process of connecting with the family; it's connecting with the village; it's connecting with the neighbors, our colleagues.

It's been seventy years since the test bombing at Trinity Site, and I think this changed everything—the way we've been living the past fast-paced seventy years. Especially here in northern New Mexico, where before these seventy years, our way of living was farming, agriculture. Making relationships through trade—who had what in what year.

"My corn grew good."

"My (whatever) grew better."

There was trade and there was really no money. When this Trinity test happened and this whole atomic age began, it just changed everything, and that's when the air, water, and land became tainted. We notice this in our health globally. We notice this in our day-to-day

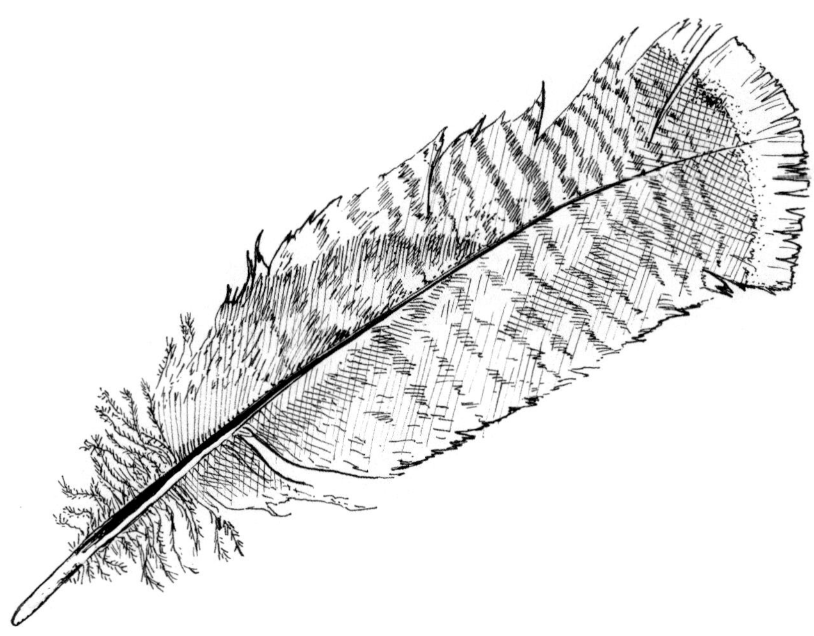

mannerisms. Indigenous people were forced into another way of living, and now we're learning that we need to remember who we are, and this isn't only for ourselves; it's a teaching from us to the world. Indigenous peoples weren't put on the face of our Mother Earth for nothing—our Creator put us in places for reasons. We are to take care of certain things—whatever can grow here, whatever animals can live here. I don't care who you are. You have roots somewhere.

Here in the United States, where the roots are so mixed and where everybody, twenty-four/seven, abides by this corporate religion, I am working diligently to make transformation and reform. It's not mine or yours. It's ours. For our own survival, all of us need to go back to some really basic things about relationships. How do we take care of one another? How do we feed one another? What is healthy for me may not be healthy for you. We need to filter through and heal things that have happened during the last seventy years. If we are people of peace, we cannot continue to praise, support, or feed things of war.

When this atomic age began, it left me in a state where I am honored to be an indigenous person. I am honored to be a member of not only a tribe but also the state of New Mexico. I am honored to be an American, but I'm also very ashamed. How do we heal? This country was the only one that used an atomic weapon on people, and it wasn't used just on the Japanese. It was used on American people right down the road, and to this day, no apology has ever been made by the leaders of this country. If you work for this, you get money. It's a not balanced psychic thing for me.

Radioactivity doesn't just go away. It's within our system now, and I cannot believe that this is not being connected to our climate change situation and all the rest of the corporate things. To me, this is the biggie.

I was fifteen years old. It was feast day. August 12. Summertime. Getting ready to prepare for the dances, I went to the creek to bathe. I stepped into the creek water, and it was really cold. I said my prayers. I started following the water, knowing that it came from the spring, from our sacred mountain. I looked up there, and there was still snow on the mountain. It was located in the Canadian zone; the mountaintop was a glacier when I was fifteen. August. Snow. It went away. So we gathered all our stories and made this nice little chart to show how the climate has changed, because we're land-based people and we witnessed this change collectively. Then we said to this foundation, "Now show us." Their chart was the same as ours. It blew them away. Blew them totally away. Our younger people were totally blown away. When you're land-based and you notice all these things and collectively share your stories on how it's been done forever, it tells you what you need to do next.

At that particular meeting, we decided we needed to save more seeds. We needed to plant more and make efforts to be more intimate in the communities. To make sure these things happen, because we're going to have many displaced people. Where are they going to go? What are they going to eat? Who are we? We were people who provided food for one another. That's who we are. So we were very conscious at that meeting. And we've been doing things consciously since.

We need to stop feeding the energies that we've been conditioned and forced to feed. When we talk negatively about activism and about protest against the atomic age, we're still feeding these energies. We need to start looking at this place as still having ancestral, spiritual energies. This is a sacred area. We need to start feeding that. What do we do when we walk up the hill for Hiroshima Days? We don't even mention the laboratory. But when we look at ancestral territory, we remember who we are. We live in the Tewa world. This Tewa world is our church. As indigenous people, we give thanks consciously, daily, from the time we get up to the time we go to bed—and we are thankful for everything that is with us. It's in the songs, it's in the dances, it's in the medicines.

So being connected and feeding that—let's see what happens. Let's start being inclusive, asking people in Santa Fe: *Can you acknowledge that you live in the Tewa world?* What does that mean to you? Just that acknowledgment is powerful, and I've been doing this for a little while now, and people's lives have changed. They want to know more—how to become more inclusive. How do I become part of this? And it's just changing your thought process and your mannerisms in life.

When I look at the bigger picture, I look at the atomic age, because it started right here in my ancestral homelands, which are very sacred. I also look at what happened here as being sacred, and you don't mess with things that are sacred. You respect them. So I look at the mannerisms of our indigenous people. We are thankful for the Creator's gifts and know what sacredness means, and we don't mess with that. We respect it.

So doing this diet is one way of feeding yourself, but you are also feeding that spirit world. That's how we take care of ourselves. So it's deeper than just following this diet. It is much deeper, and it opened up a whole new thought process on what needs to be done to continue on.

INDEX

 The Museum of New Mexico Press is a division of the New Mexico Department of Cultural Affairs.

Director: Anna Gallegos
Editorial director: Lisa Pacheco
Art & production director: David Skolkin
Designed by Ann Lowe

Composition: Set in Nueva Std and Gill Sans
Manufactured in China
10 9 8 7 6 5 4

Library of Congress Cataloging-in-Publication Data
Names: Swentzell, Roxanne, 1962- editor. | Perea, Patricia M., editor.
Title: The Pueblo food experience cookbook : whole food of our ancestors / edited by Roxanne Swentzell and Patricia M. Perea, original drawings by Roxanne Swentzell.
Description: Santa Fe : Museum of New Mexico Press, [2016] | Includes index.
Identifiers: LCCN 2016023716 | ISBN 9780890136195 (hardcover : alk. paper)
Subjects: LCSH: Pueblo cooking. | Cooking, American--Southwestern style. | Pueblo Indians--Food. | LCGFT: Cookbooks.
Classification: LCC TX715.2.S69 P84 2016 | DDC 641.5979--dc23 LC record available at https://lccn.loc.gov/2016023716

ISBN 978-0-89013-619-5 hardcover
Museum of New Mexico Press
PO Box 2087
Santa Fe, New Mexico 87504
mnmpress.org

Front cover: Roxanne Swentzell, *Tamales.*
Back cover: Roxanne Swentzell, *Tse-ping* (belly-button, center place, emergence, home, connection to source), 1991. Photograph by Craig Smith. Courtesy of the Heard Museum.
This sculpture is of a family eating around one bowl filled with seeds. The bowl is symbolic of the Earth showing the mountains and valleys in Pueblo patterns. The family are all humans nourished by the gifts of the Earth, symbolized by the seeds that represent our future. One Earth, one family, one future.—Roxanne Swentzell

Pages vi, 53, 86, 89: Photographs by Kitty Leaken. Used with permission.
Page 83: Photograph by Charlie McDonald, former Region 3 Regional Botanist. Courtesy of the USDA.
All other color photographs by Roxanne Swentzell and other PFE participants.
All black-and-white photographs courtesy of the Palace of the Governors Photo Archives (NMHM/DCA).